AF305245

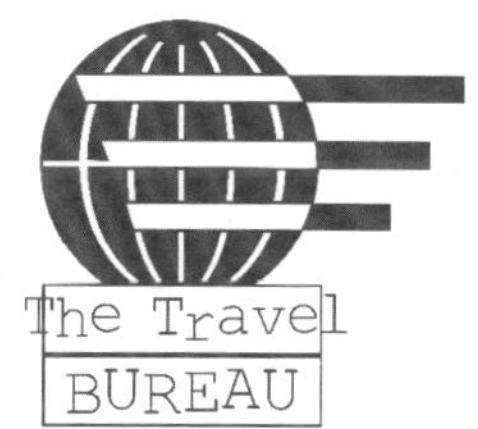
The Travel
BUREAU

The Travel Bureau

Paulina Olowska selects from the Christen Sveaas Art Foundation

Christen Sveaas'
Kunststiftelse

Whitechapel
Gallery

Introduction

I still remember the time when travel agents would bring tickets and boarding passes to your home before a vacation, when smoking was still permitted on planes and when you could show up to your flight only minutes before departure. Today, the traditional travel bureau is long gone, having been replaced by e-tickets, Expedia and Google. The travel bureau was not only a place of transaction. It was a place of knowledge and mapping out of dream journeys. A revolution has transpired, and while the world has gotten smaller and every one of its corners has become more accessible, the distance between people has perhaps increased. Travel was about escape, yet today the traces we leave behind on social media are almost as important as the moments cherished, the discoveries made and the monuments visited that we travelled so far to discover. As with everything Paulina Olowska engages with, she chooses the perfect time to draw our attention to a phenomenon, to remind us of its essence, the true value and the finer nuances that perhaps got lost on the way. The Covid-19 pandemic has brought travel as we knew it to an abrupt stop. What better way to pause and reflect on the movement of people and ideas than to travel through Olowska's selection of works displayed at the Whitechapel Gallery.

Norwegians have always been a travelling people, from the Norse Vikings who were the first to discover Vinland and the Americas, the wave of Norwegian immigrants who followed in the footsteps of their ancestors, seeking the American dream in the early twentieth century, the pioneering Polar explorers Fridtjof Nansen and Roald Amundsen to Thor Heyerdahl's adventures and explorations on the Pacific Seas proving that people from South America could have reached Polynesia as early as pre-Columbian times. Norwegian artists have also been bound to travel, often to Copenhagen or Paris as part of their artistic training, or further afield for inspiration and new ideas. Both Johannes Rian and Thore Heramb, whose works are included in the present selection, were greatly influenced by their trips to France in the 1930s, '40s and '50s. And while their palette changed to warmer hues, most of these artworks have remained in Norwegian collections. It is therefore especially moving that Olowska shines a spotlight on these works.

Artists have always been adventurers and explorers of the mind. Through their eyes we see places and situations in a new light. The current selection of works also evidences the ability of abstract work to bring us to unknown places, whether it is the gates of heaven in Gillian Ayres' miniature work *Hark Hark the Lark*, or Charline von Heyl's *Stationmaster*. We are extremely proud that Olowska embarked on this journey and equally enthused to share her work with the Norwegian audience when her major solo exhibition opens to the public on 30 April 2022 at Kistefos Museum. This exhibition will consider and explore the notion of hauntology through her painting, performance and installations.

In 1996, Christen Sveaas founded the Kistefos Museum, situated an hour outside Oslo along the Rand River. It was originally intended to be an industrial heritage museum dedicated to preserving the intact pulp press mill erected by his grandfather in 1889. However, his interest in art quickly led him to shift focus while staying true to and honouring the industrial framework and its distinct identity. Today, the museum boasts two temporary exhibition spaces dedicated to contemporary art, alongside almost fifty outdoor sculptures dotted around the dramatic landscape. We hope your next travel will bring you to Kistefos.

Our sincere thanks to Paulina Olowska for making this exhibition happen and to the Whitechapel Gallery under the leadership of Iwona Blazwick for setting the course for the thrilling collection displays here in London.

William Flatmo, Director
Christen Sveaas Art Foundation

Where Shall We Go?

Who has gazed at an image of a palm-fringed beach, a sunlit mountaintop or a glamorous metropolis and not dreamt of escape? This longing was once encapsulated by the travel bureau, decorated with alluring posters of places that were anywhere but here. The travel agent; the chic flight attendant; a couple laughing in front of the Eiffel Tower, serenaded by a Venetian gondolier or walking through the surf – these were the characters that once occupied our travel fantasies.

That ache of desire and the fantastical destinations we imagine become all the more intense when we feel economically or socially trapped. Perhaps analogous with the utopian dream of travel is the utopian dream of communist and capitalist societies – both offering future ideals of social or individual fulfilment, both failing. It was the former that framed the memories of artist Paulina Olowska, who was born in Poland in 1976. Olowska recounts regular teenage visits to Orbis, the largest and oldest travel agency in Poland. *The idea of entering such an office was already travel.*

Olowska references what French anthropologist Marc Augé termed the 'non-place' – a space such as an airport or a shopping mall.[1] Unlike a home or a workplace, such spaces do not define identity but offer the possibility of leaving it behind. They are stage sets for anonymous interactions, the promise of new destinations, new looks, new tomorrows, deftly stewarded by helpful professionals. Olowska recounts how the futures that the Orbis bureau once promised were also encapsulated in poster designs featuring the graphic panache that made Polish poster art famous in the 1960s and '70s.[2] *[They had] very strong visual content, like a cute spaniel puppy in a bag…or a sparrow dressed in a suit with a suitcase'. [You] really felt that you could travel*

1   Marc Augé, *Non-places: Introduction to an Anthropology of Supermodernity* (London: Verso, 1992).
2   Andrea Austoni, 'The Legacy of Polish Posters', *Smashing Magazine* (17 January 2010) (www.smashingmagazine.com/2010/01/the-legacy-of-polish-poster-design).

*just by looking at the posters. This made me realise that using sets
and theatrical devices in my shows is a way to present works,
especially painting. Like the theatrical set, it makes you look from
another angle.'*

Olowska has created environments that are like stage sets
or backdrops for magazine shoots. Described as 'folk-futuristic',
there's a period quality to the interiors she creates, as if their
elegant colours and modernist graphics channel the hopes of
a different era. A salon-café she established with artist Lucy
McKenzie in Warsaw in 2003 was called the Nova Popularna and
evoked legendary bars such as La Coupole in Paris or the Cedar
Tavern in New York, where avant-garde artists and writers would
congregate. In existence for just one month, it was welcoming and
convivial – a proposal that asked, what if such a lovely place could
really exist? The artist describes how *'the whole place looked like
a dream scene where bartenders, guests and the design united to
evoke the memory of a Post-Impressionist painting or a place for
avant-garde meetings.'*

Painting is a consistent feature of Olowska's multifac-
eted practice. In another collaboration with McKenzie at the
Kunstverein Braunschweig in 2004, she created a stage set for
McKenzie's story *Desky Maidens*, featuring portraits of female
icons of modernism – Djuna Barnes, Vanessa Bell, Nina Hamnett,
Charlotte Perriand and Virginia Woolf. But she also continues to
depict with illustrative precision anonymous fashionably dressed
and coiffed women posing against a glamorous background,
redolent of another age. In Olowska's cosmology, women are the
ideal heroines and protagonists of a temporality that draws on
the past but offers a vision of the future. Her openness to working
with other artists and her skill in creating remarkable mise-en-
scènes made her an ideal candidate to curate one episode of a
four-part celebration of the Christen Sveaas Art Foundation at
Whitechapel Gallery.

*'Looking through the works in the Christen Sveaas
Art Foundation, I was looking through the eye of a journey.
Looking at paintings as a metaphor of longing, wishing to be
somewhere else…'*

Perhaps the beginning of that curatorial journey could
be a work from 2018 by Monica Bonvicini. Floating on a white
background, mirrored letters read simply 'Same Old Shit', while
offering a perfect reflection of viewers' faces. From there, we might
peak over the top of the outspread newspaper in the lightbox
transparency *Sunday Sun 1937* (2012) to find Rodney Graham
in bed, indulging in perhaps the most modest form of escape –
laughing at the funny pages. Laura Owens has already read and
disposed of her newspaper and used it to clean her brushes in a
gigantic canvas where news items long dispatched to oblivion are
overlaid with dabs of colour that suggest the creation of a future
work of art.

A painting by Olowska features a young woman wearing
a boldly patterned couture summer dress; she sits in a meadow
full of daisies, a cottage on the horizon rising above a field of
wheat. The title reveals this is a mannequin in a window display
of the famous Soviet department store GUM, itself a nod to the
aspirations of Western capitalism, the tableau a wistful emblem
of spring in an Eastern European winter. Windows often feature
in art as symbols of another world. The windows evoked by Julia
Rommel's *Ex-husband* (2018) propose actual escape. She inserts
two pale blue and white 'windows' framing an expansive rose
madder monochrome. Above the rectangular frames, triangles
of pale blue and pink are edged off the canvas. The structure and
palette, reminiscent of clapboard houses, combine with the soap
opera–like title to suggest new domestic horizons.

The patterns in Fredrik Værslev's *Untitled* (2018) similarly
evoke homeliness. Against a linen coloured background, he
block-prints red, blue and green wavy stripes, dancing arcs of
ears of corn, bands and polka dots that might decorate a tea
towel. The patterns flow upwards together as if in a Proustian
reminiscence of grandma's linen cupboard. Ida Ekblad also
channels the domestic with her painting *The Proofreader* (2017),
a geometric composition of red, blue, white and green rectangles
gaily patterned with rosettes and bunches of marigolds. This
domestic register is also captured in a porcelain urn hand-made
by Skuja Braden and titled *Ima Woman* (2020). Moving from

décor to eros, the vase features two young women locked in an embrace, their lips fused in a kiss. Like female genies in a bottle, they evoke a wishful Sapphic congress.

Brian Alfred's little 2005 collage of the Hollywood sign also represents the horizon of desire, an aspirational launch pad for fame and fortune. Glamour similarly beckons in Arne Ekeland's *Møte i porten* (Meeting at the gate) (1965), where a mosaic of diamonds in purple, gold, lime and violet offer a mirage of two figures stepping out in a shimmering vision of finery.

Metaphors for journeys appear in paintings such as Charline von Heyl's *Stationmaster* (2013), where structuring geometries of black and brown frame graphic signs and gestural marks that suggest the expressive release of language and physical movement. The idea of take-off also resonates in Pierre et Gilles' self-portraits as cosmonauts, festooned with flowers and ready for space travel. Also just setting off is Marina Abramović seated on a white stallion and holding a large white flag. The subtitle of her photograph *The Hero* (2001), *(Family story of my father who was a hero in the Second World War in Yugoslavia)*, situates her as the dynastic heroine of an ongoing political struggle, embarking on an epic adventure.

Arrival in dreamt-of destinations comes with paintings such as Oluf Wold-Torne's 1913 oil painting of a sailboat and boat-house on the shores of the coastal town of Holmsbu in his native Norway. Thore Heramb's *Landskapskomposisjon* (Landscape composition) (1958) offers a joyful immersion in the kinesis of cloud, sky, forest, fjord and rocky escarpment distilling the landscape into a riot of vivid colour.

Getting lost in the natural world is also powerfully evoked in Gillian Ayres' *Hark Hark the Lark* (1984–90). Her exuberant squiggles, blobs and dashes of orange, sky-blue, coral, lime and yellow that overflow from the canvas onto its black frame give synaesthetic expression to the song and the skydiving exultance of the lark. By contrast, Ed Ruscha's *Mountain Standard* (2000), one of a series of paintings he made at the turn of the century featuring hyperreal images of mountain ranges, encapsulates a distant and detached version of a snow-capped mountain. A white silhouette cuts a triangular void across the front of this painting, based on a stock photograph. It's as if this were a graphic to be used in an ad for menthol cigarettes, or a gas station, or perhaps a cowboy film. Ruscha combines transcendence with banality, the sublime as commodity experience, in his evocations of the American dream.

Settling into the holiday mood, Johannes Rian's *Spansk restaurant* (Spanish restaurant) (1949) is a composition of pure pleasure. A Matisse-like odalisque gazes at the viewer flanked by epicurean delights in a sumptuously decorated interior, the silhouettes of wine bottles echoing the figure's dark hair, eyes and skirt with intoxicating languor. Hurvin Anderson takes us to a Caribbean beach with *Blue and Gold Umbrella* (1994). This tiny horizontal frieze featuring the tops of four overlapping sunshades vibrates with heat and light, a fragment that powerfully evokes the white sands at their feet. Rosson Crow also plunges us into mesmeric heat with *Relics of the Truth Tellers* (2017), a cinematically scaled painting and photomontage of a Californian desert scape. Gigantic cactuses growing amongst the telegraph poles and detritus of a desert wasteland are cast in hallucinogenic fluorescent pink.

We enter the realm of what could be drug-induced ecstasy with Berta Fischer's 2016 *Xurla*, an extravagant cluster of polychrome acrylic sheets. Flailing outwards from the wall in transparent shades of neon orange, scarlet and pea green, her work has been described by critic Charity Coleman as 'the happy wreckage of a good party'.

As we end this narrative, things get darker. Till Gerhard's 2007 *Black Hole/Sun* depicts a chasm that has opened up besides an idyllic campsite in a sunny pine forest. From its depths, spirits of paint emerge to obliterate the campers. The forest features in myth and fairy tale as both Arcadian and hostile, a place of disorientation and threat. Jakob Weidemann's 1961 painting *Fra Skogen* – From the Forest – has a dark brooding palette of murky pine, blood red, purple and brown evoking formless atavistic fears. In a scene that is at once a source of wonder and anxiety, Caragh Thuring's surreal *Night* (2017) features the full moon as an eye

illuminating and witnessing a pyramid erupting like a volcano
and pouring molten lava towards the silhouette of a submarine
emerging from the sea.

And so we must return to the Travel Bureau having jour-
neyed from the horizons of desire to the panic of being lost, under
the aegis of Paulina Olowska's complex curatorial vision. In this
installation she also reveals the true nature of the gallery as a
waiting room offering portals to other destinations. As with all her
installations, 'The Travel Bureau' is, in its entirety, a work of art.

Iwona Blazwick, Director
Whitechapel Gallery

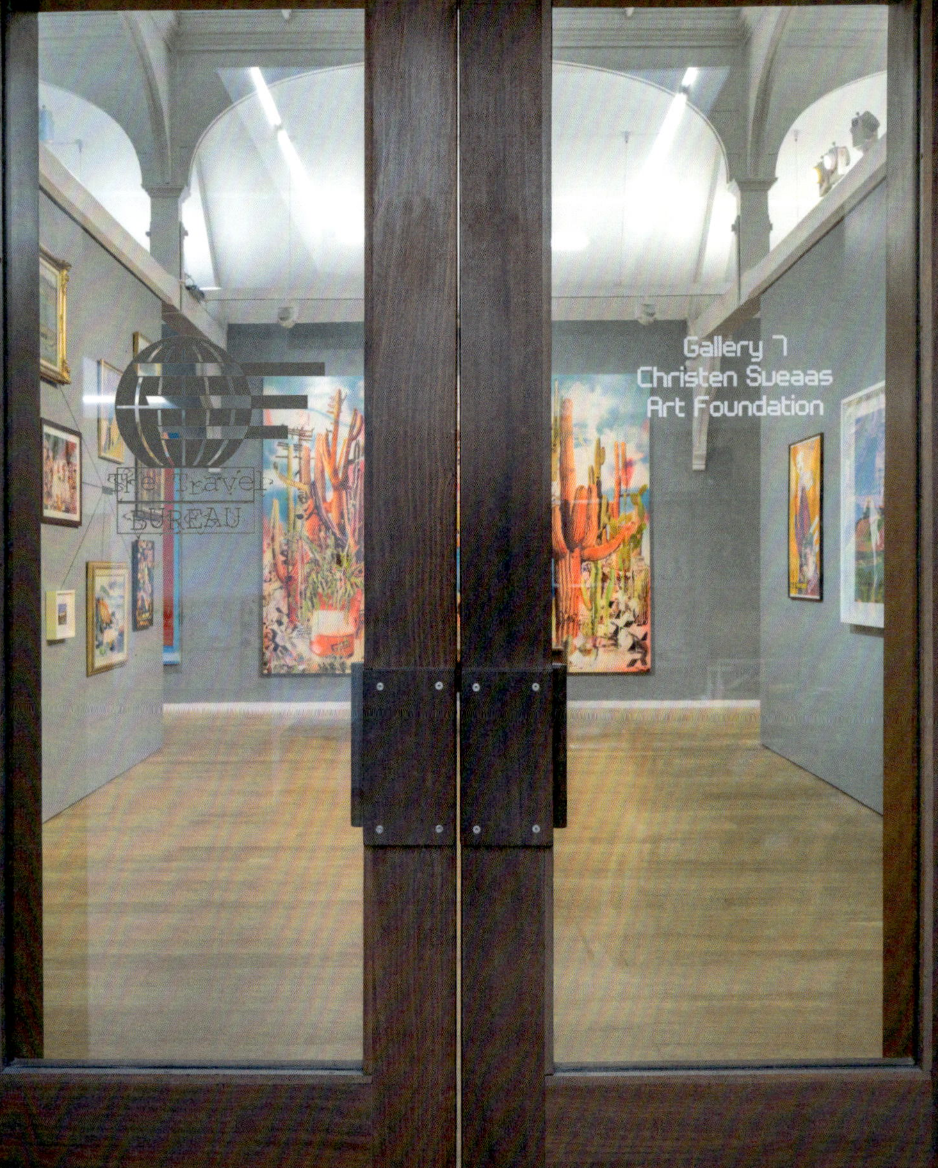
The Travel BUREAU
Gallery 7
Christen Sueaas
Art Foundation

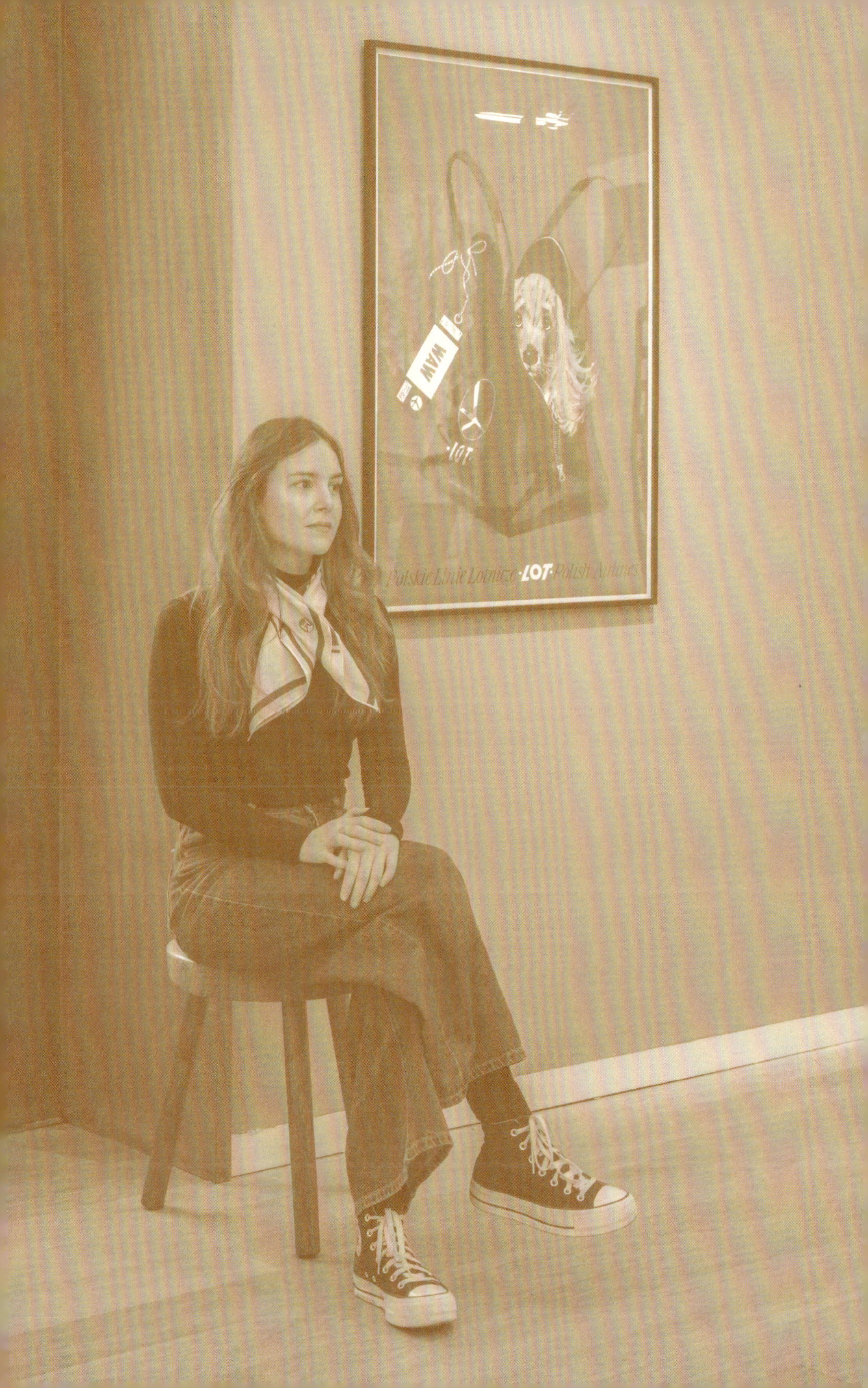

WAW
·LOT·
Polskie Linie Lotnicze ·LOT· Polish Airlines

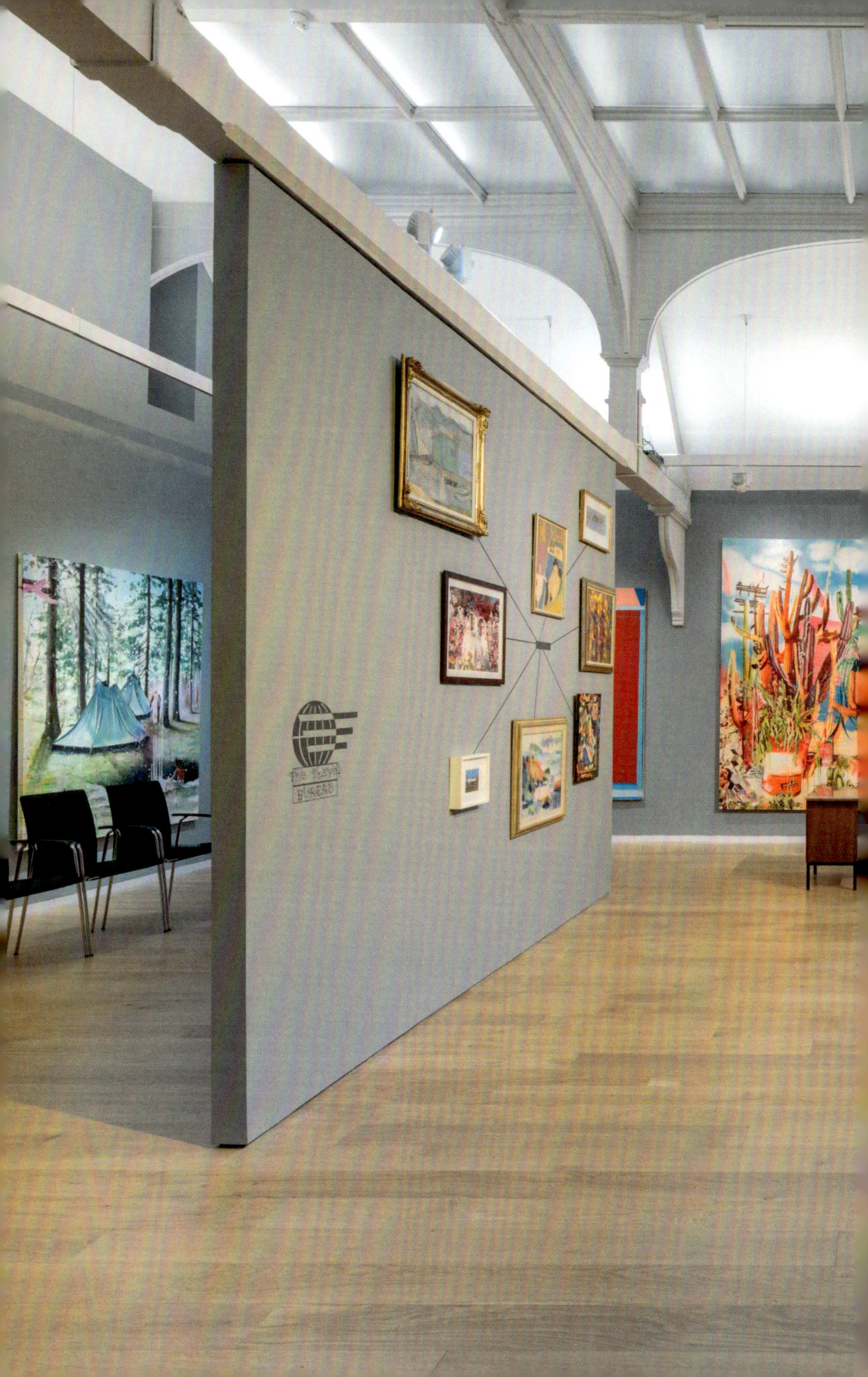

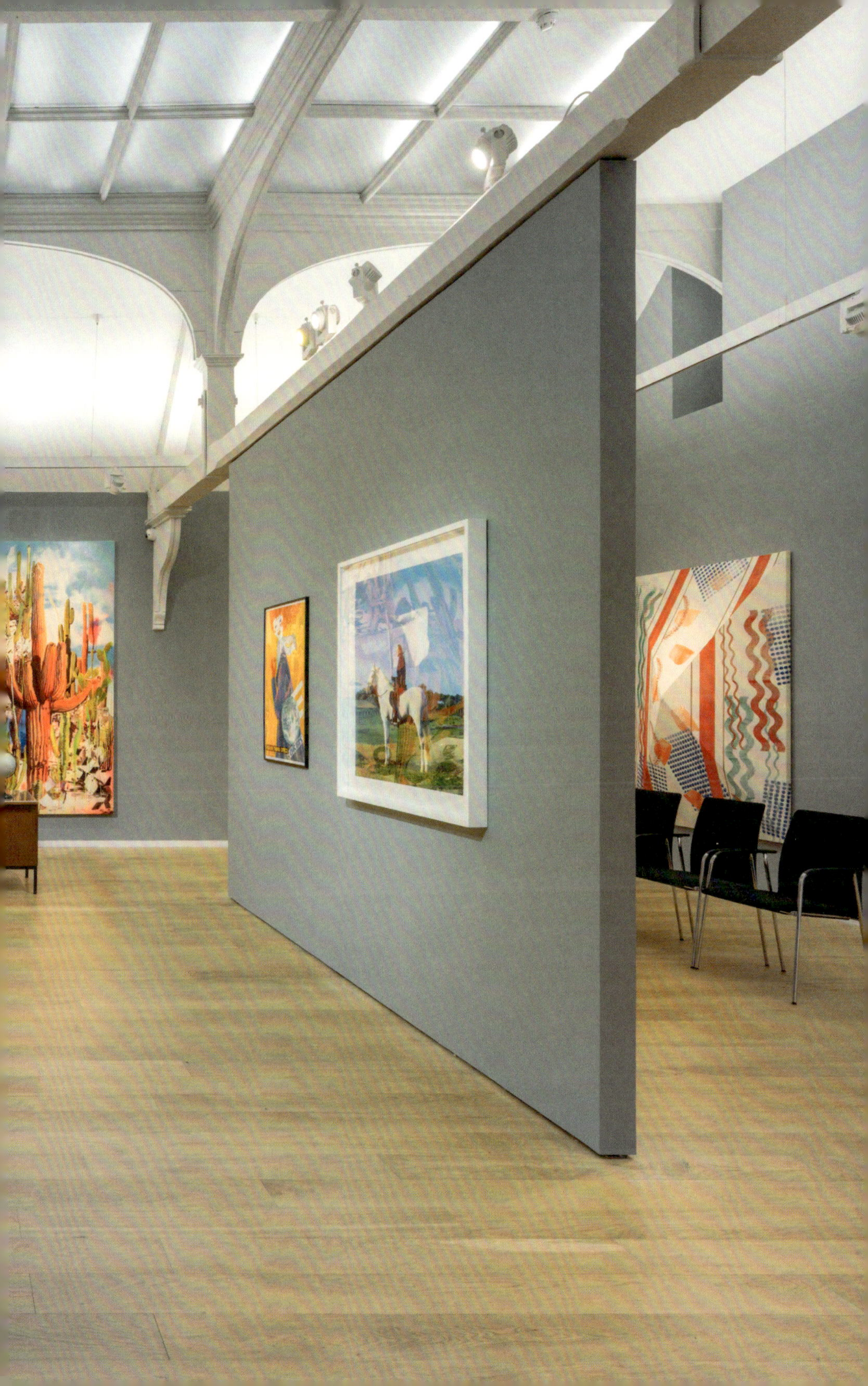

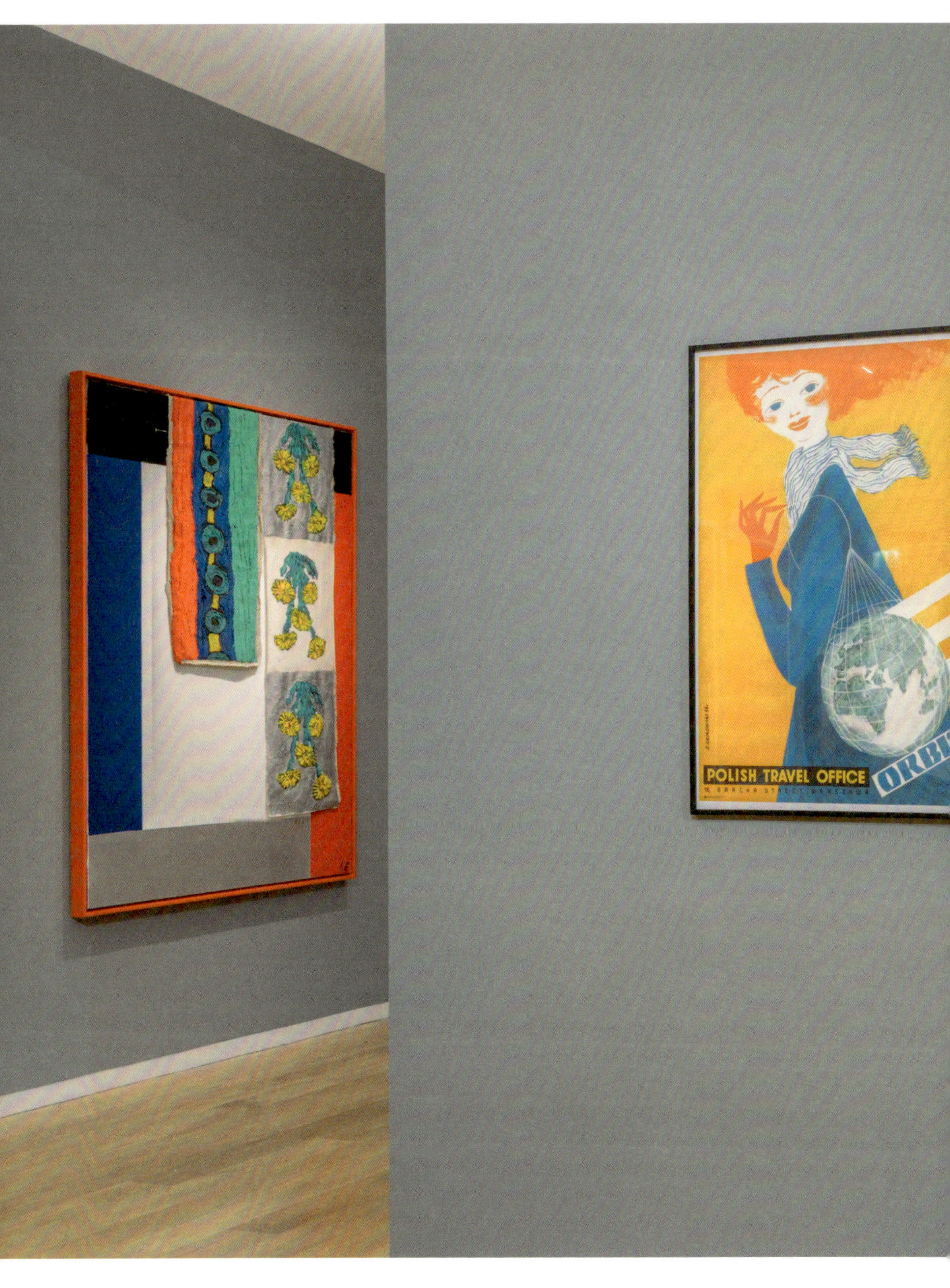
POLISH TRAVEL OFFICE
ORBI

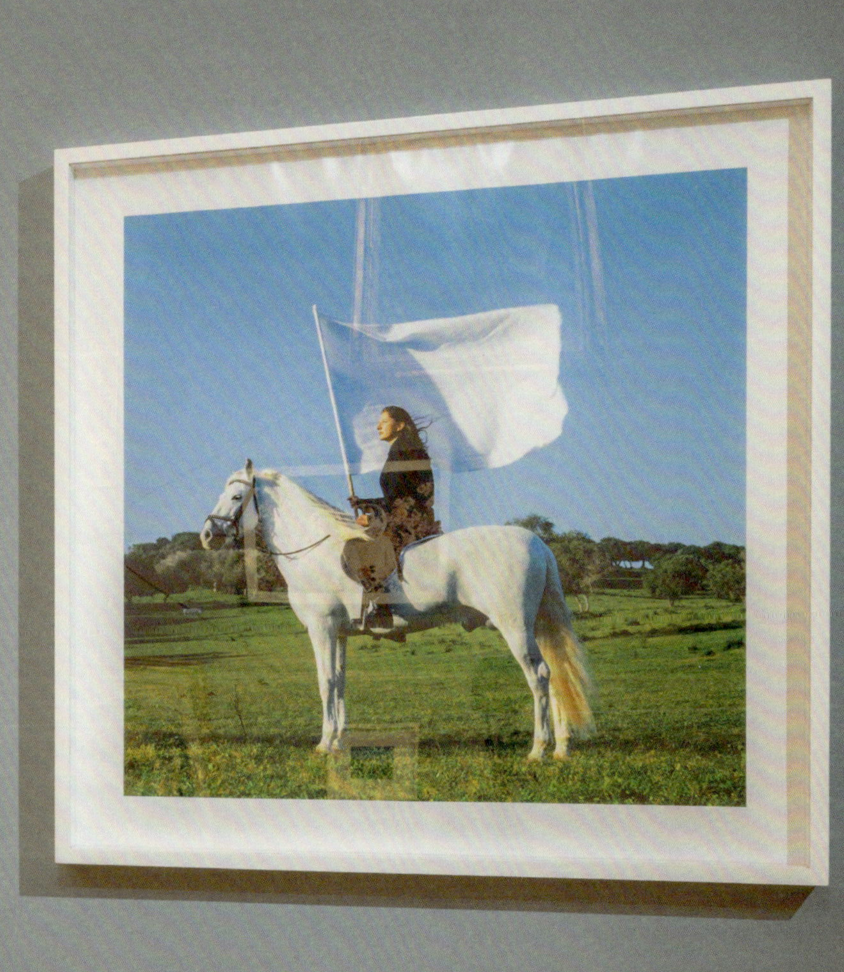

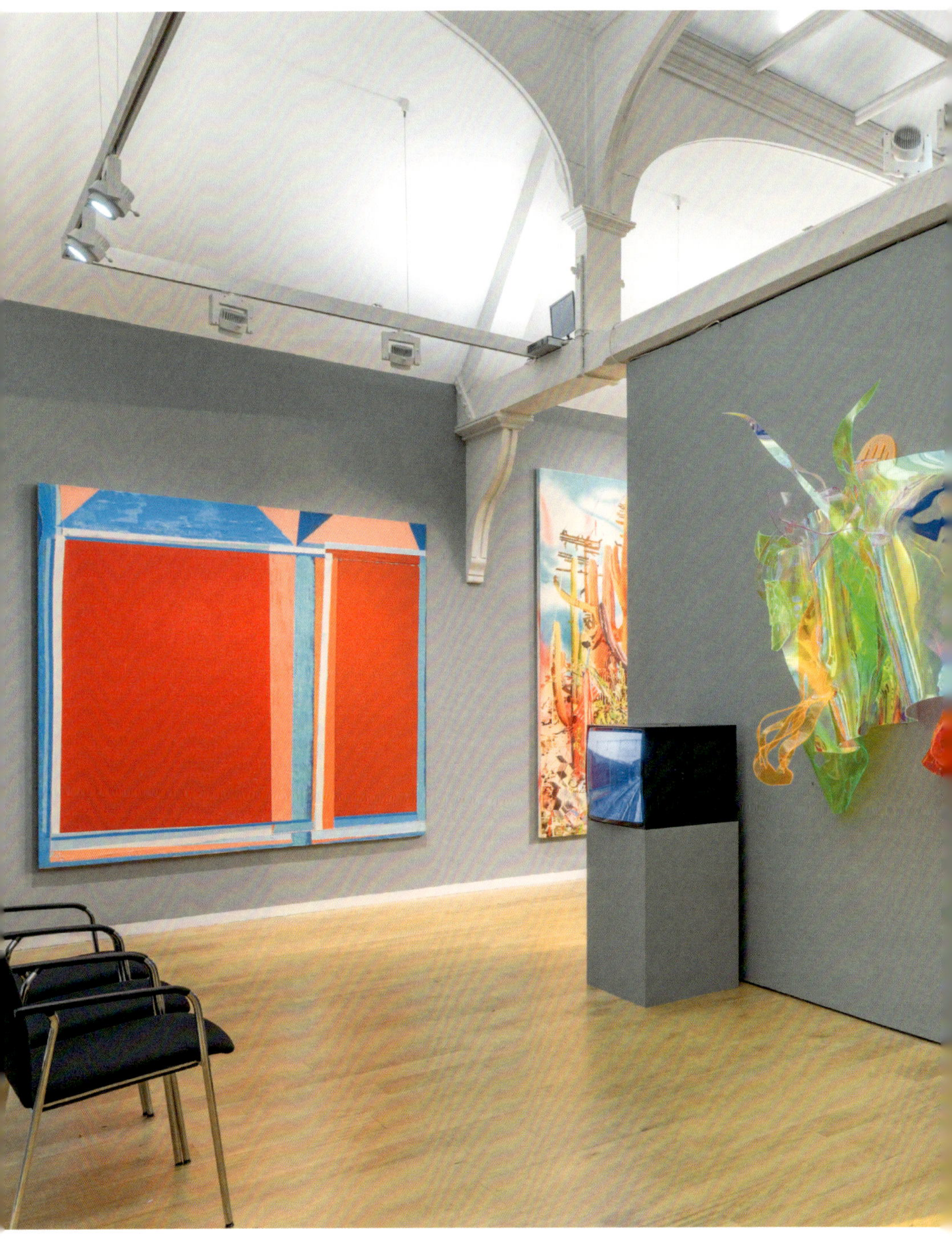

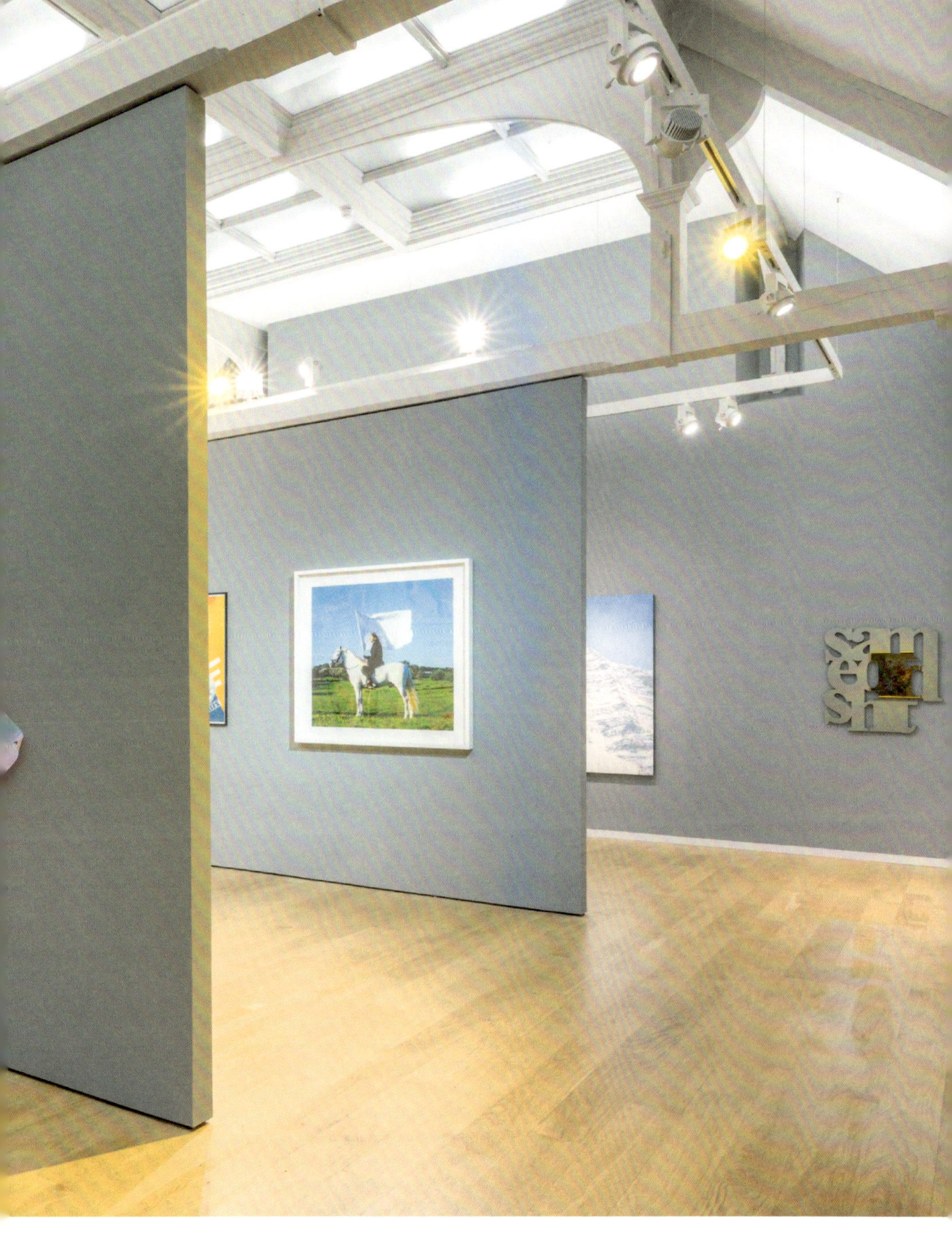

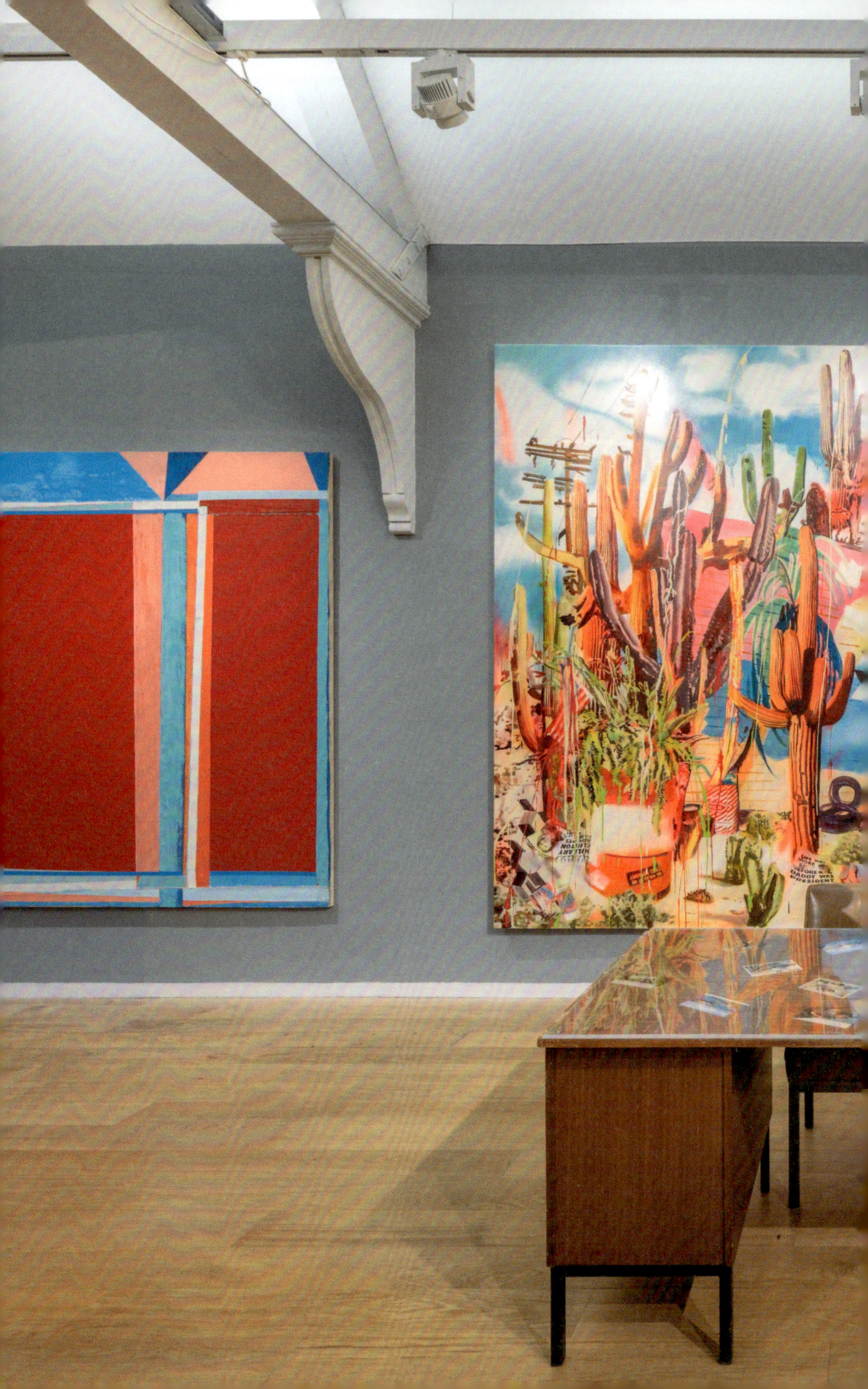

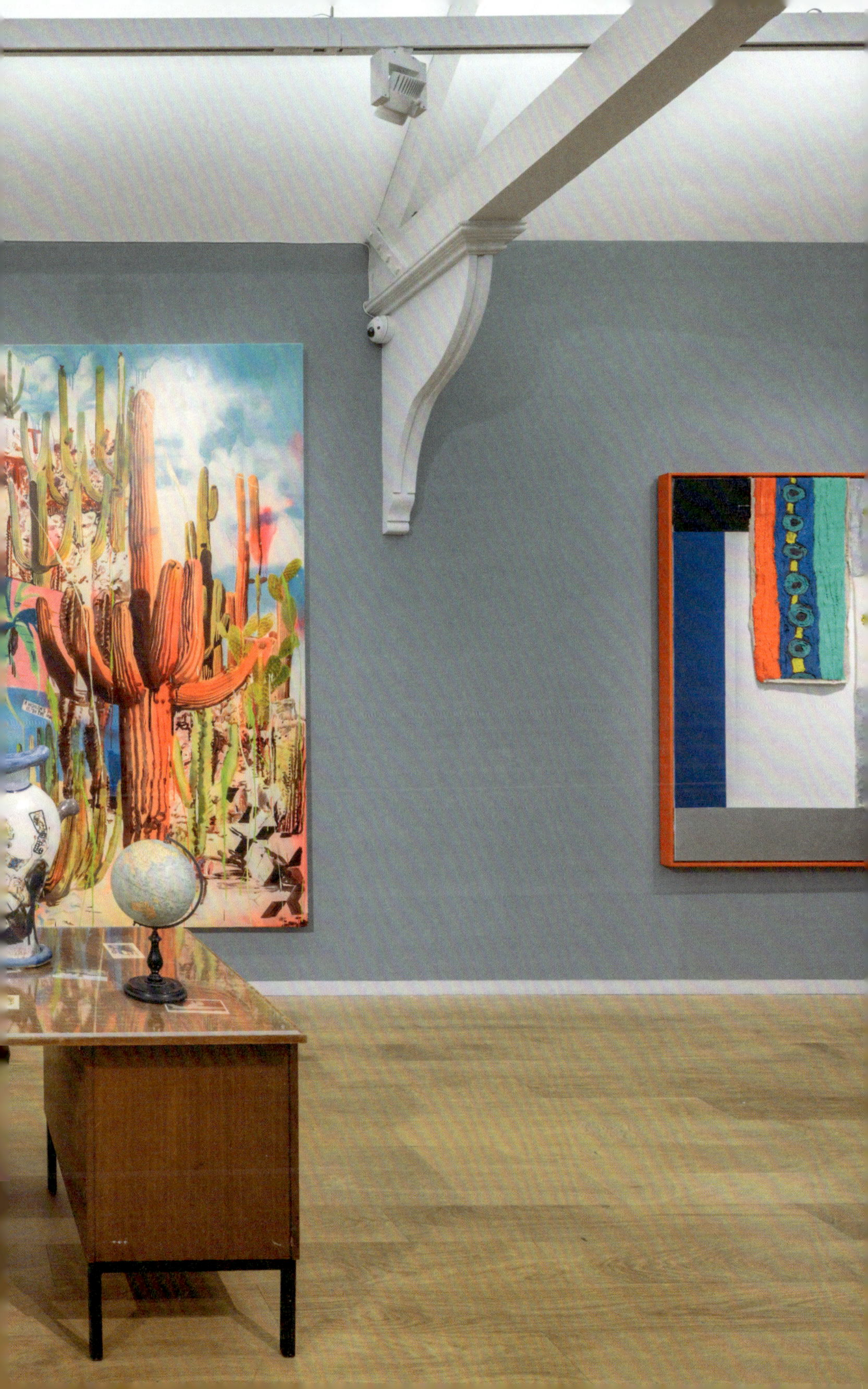

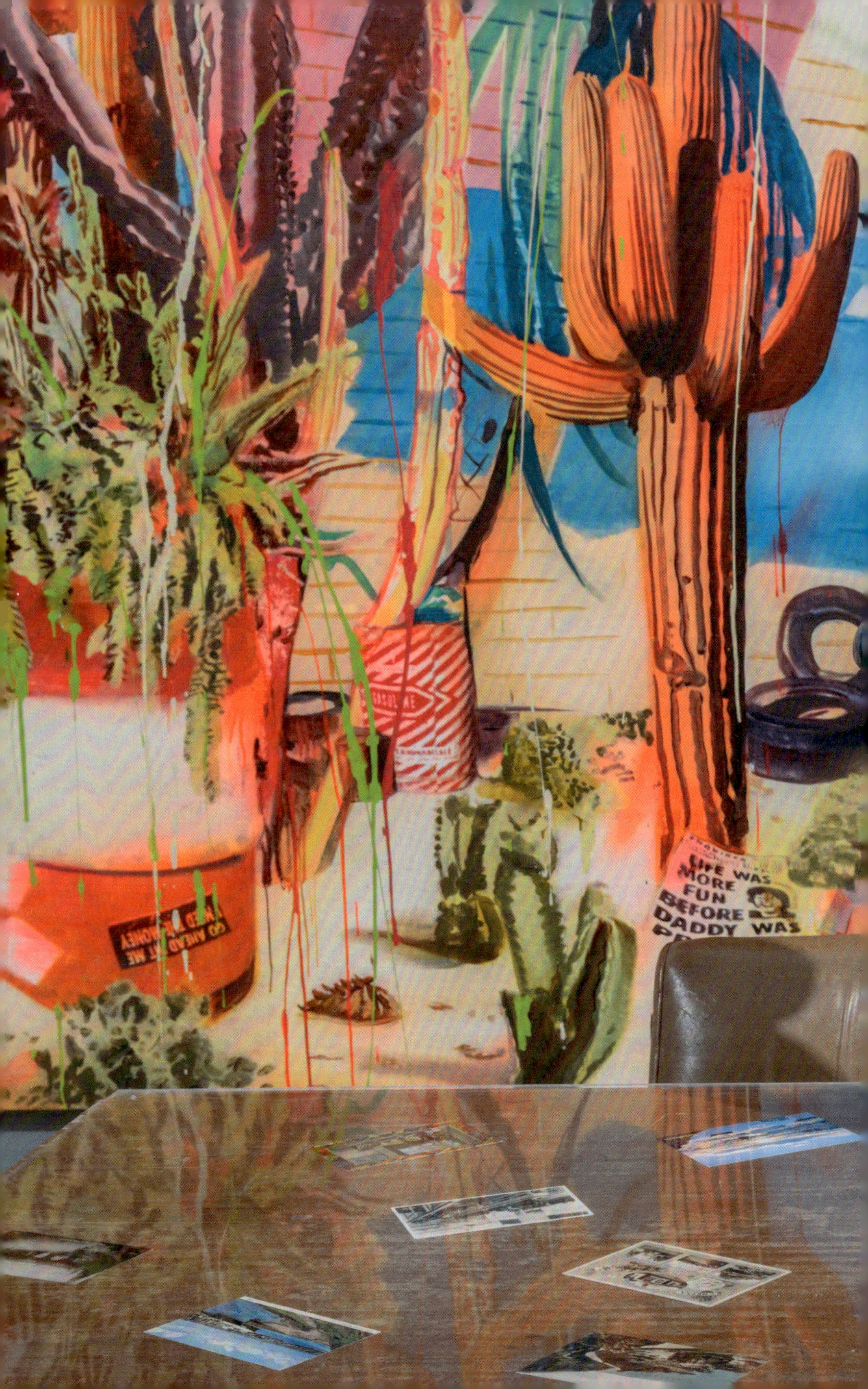
GASOLINE
GO AHEAD TAKE MY MONEY
LIFE WAS
MORE
FUN
BEFORE
DADDY WAS

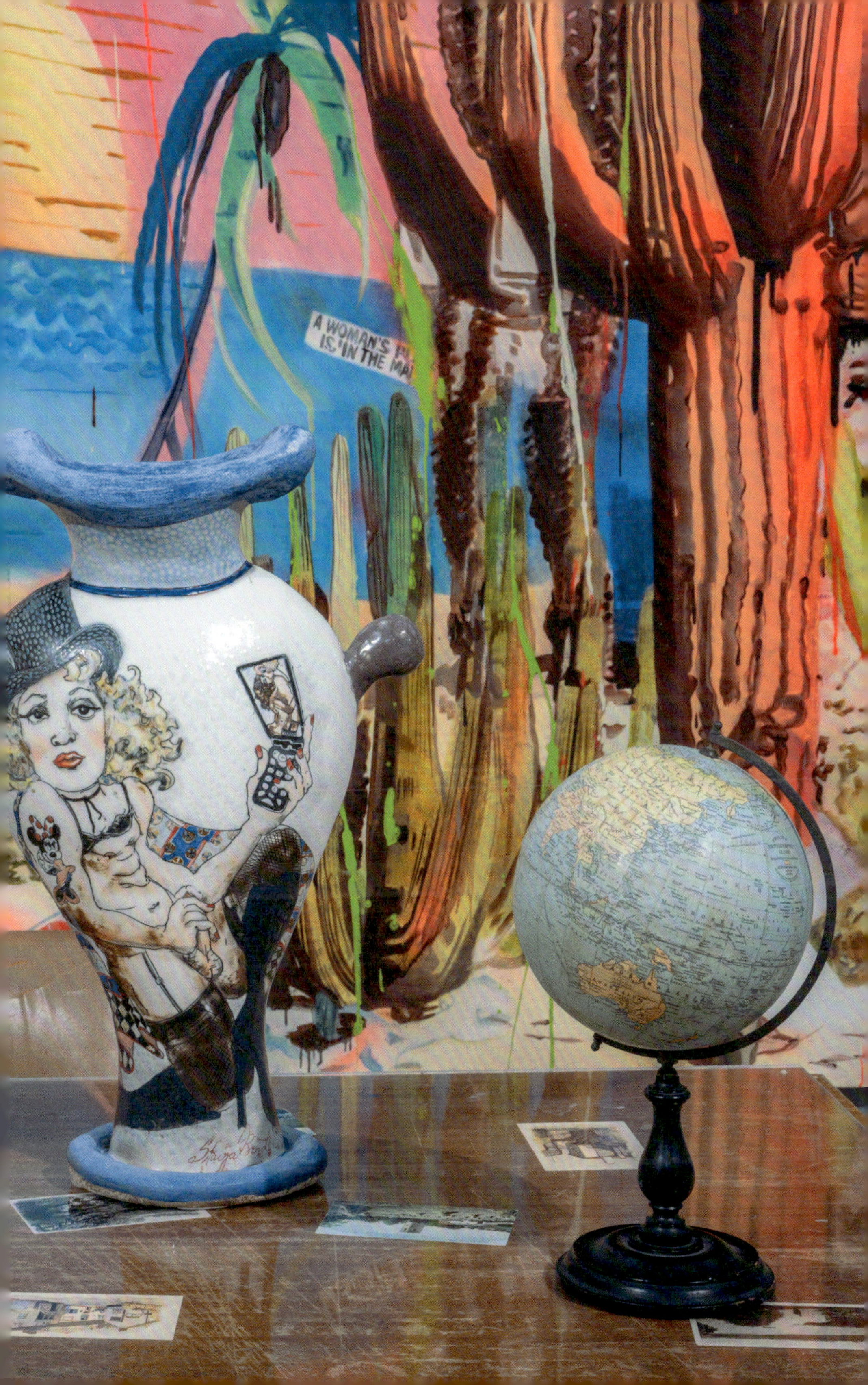

A WOMAN'S P
IS IN THE MA

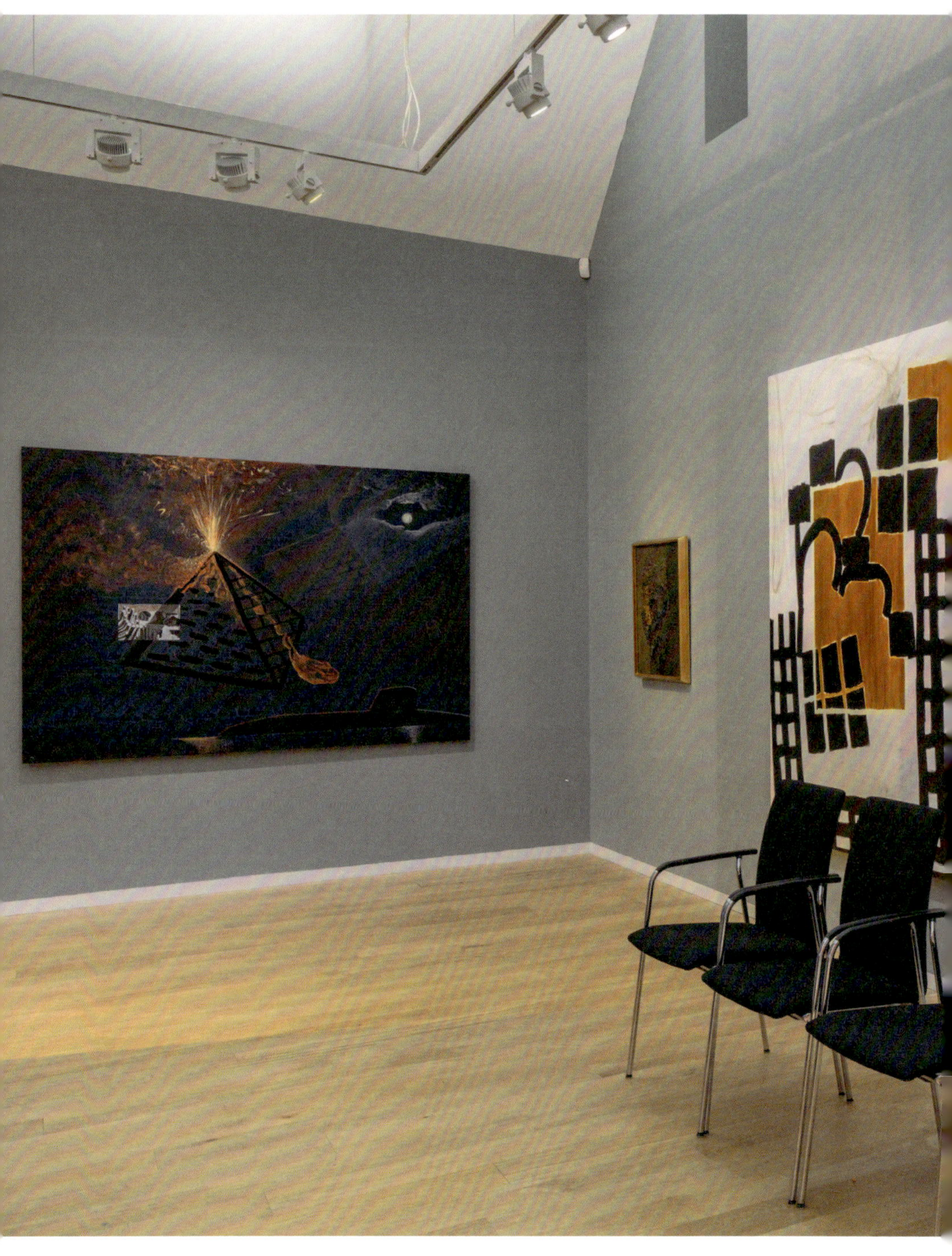

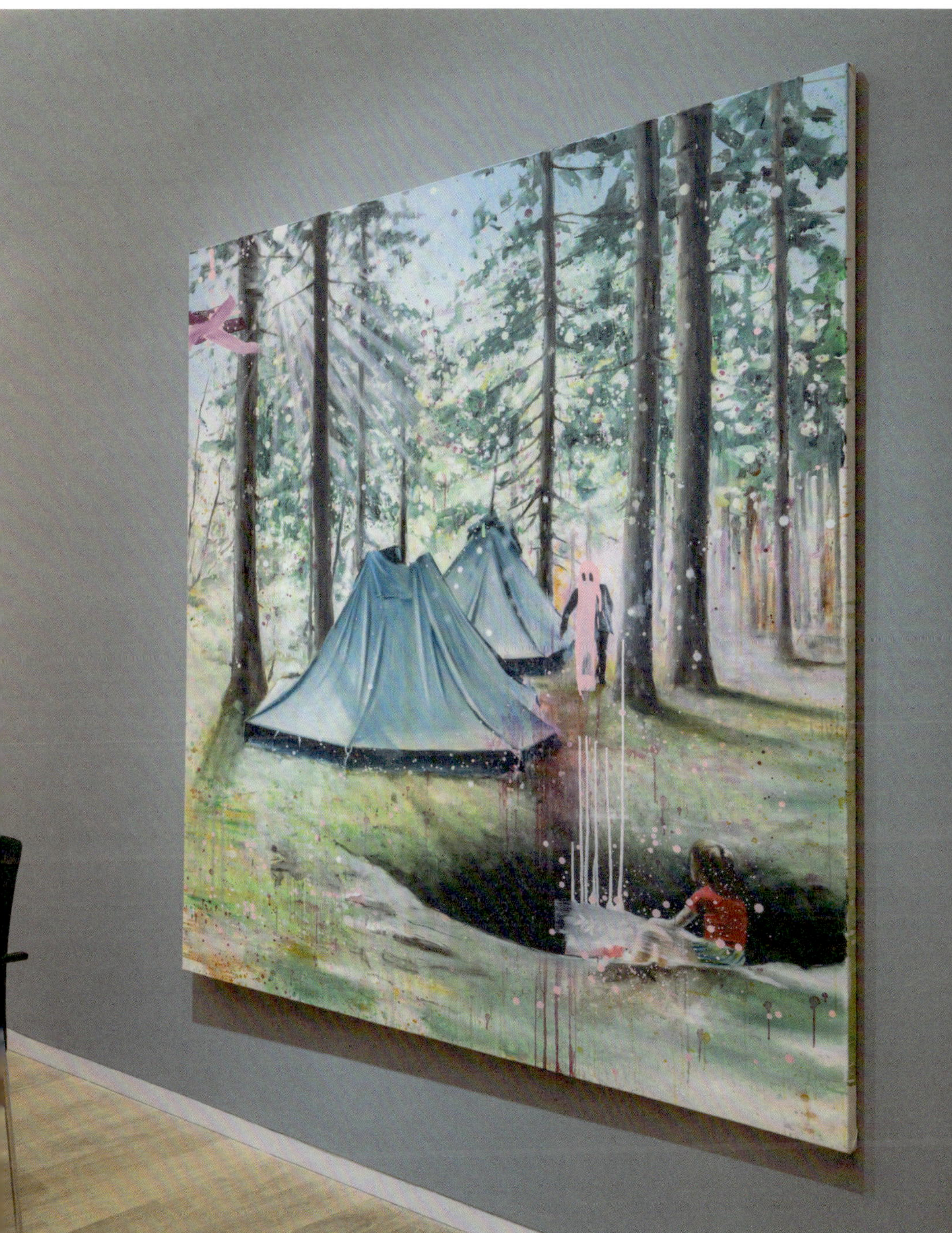

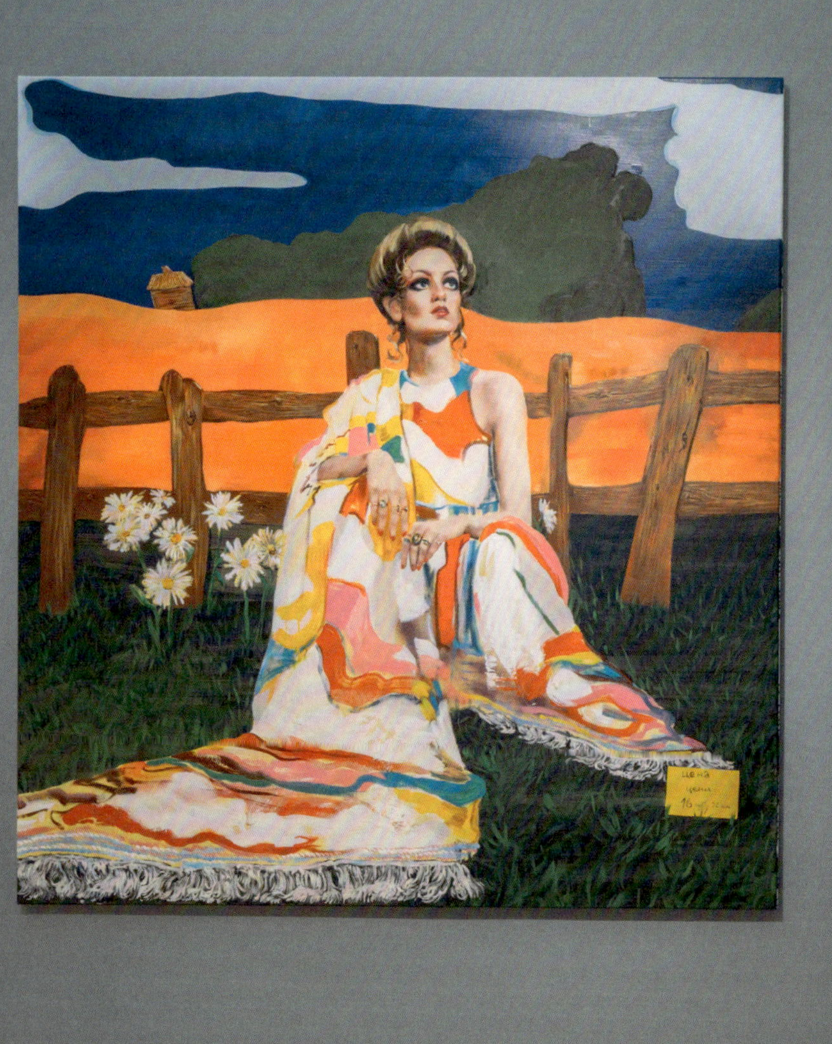

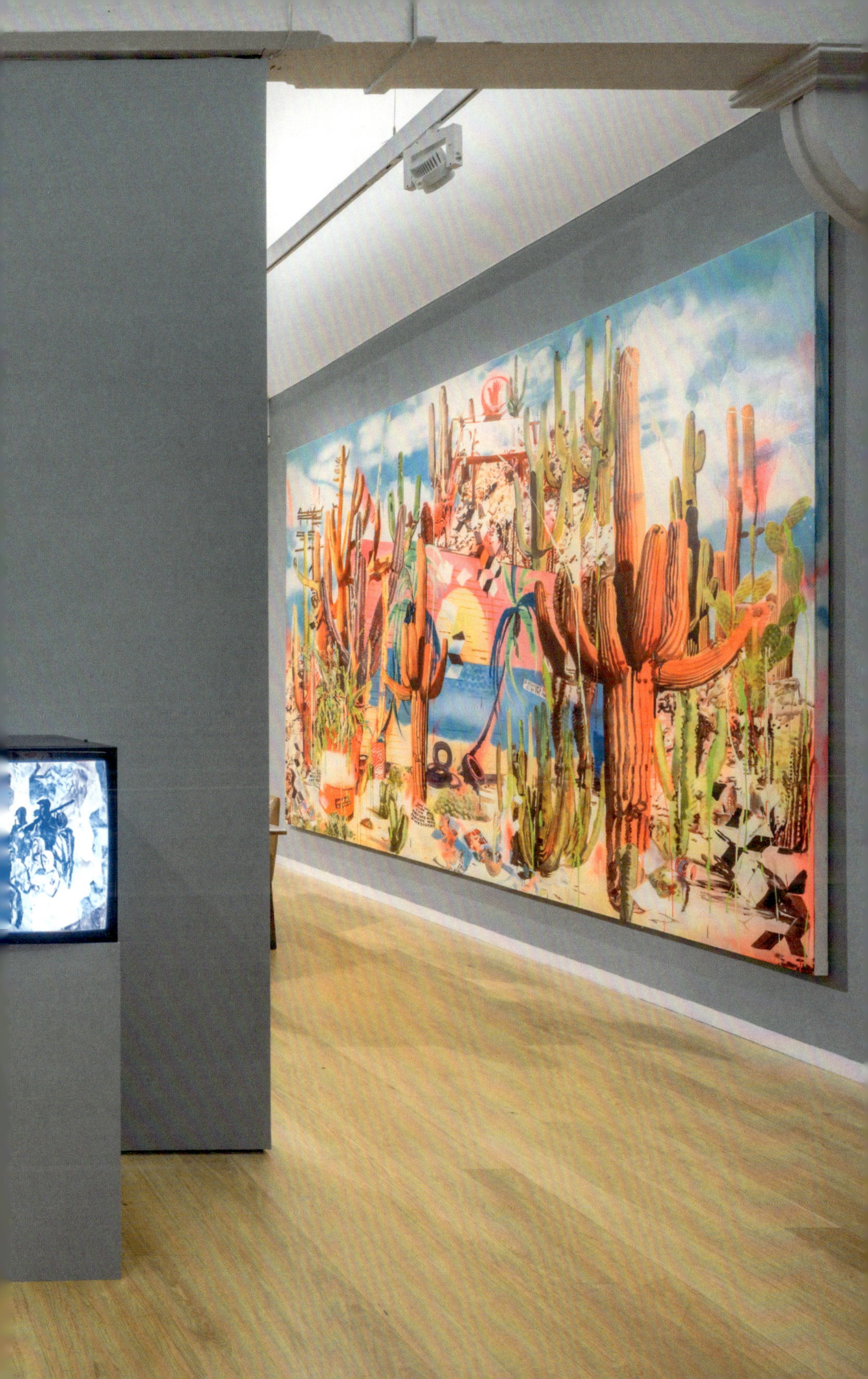

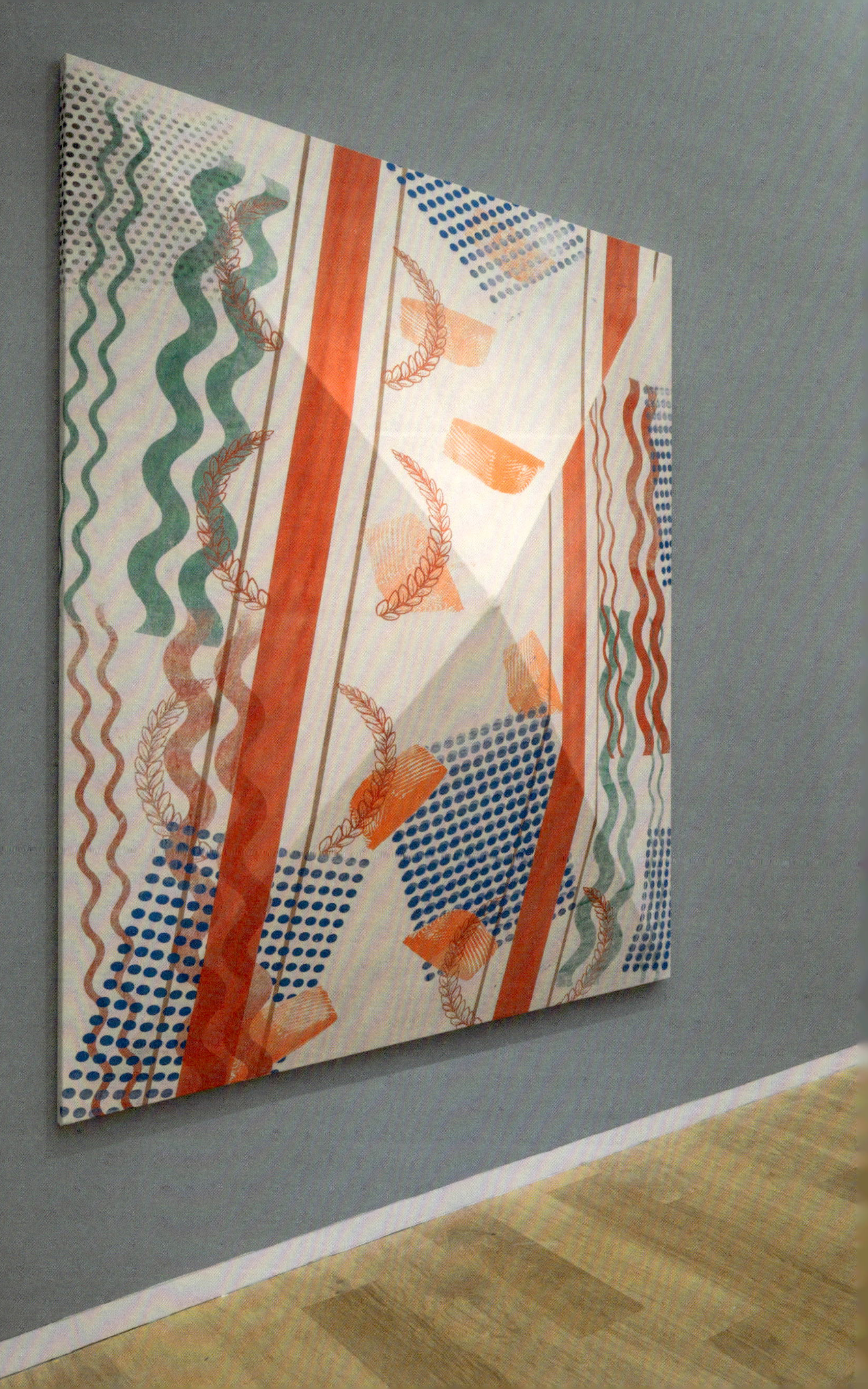

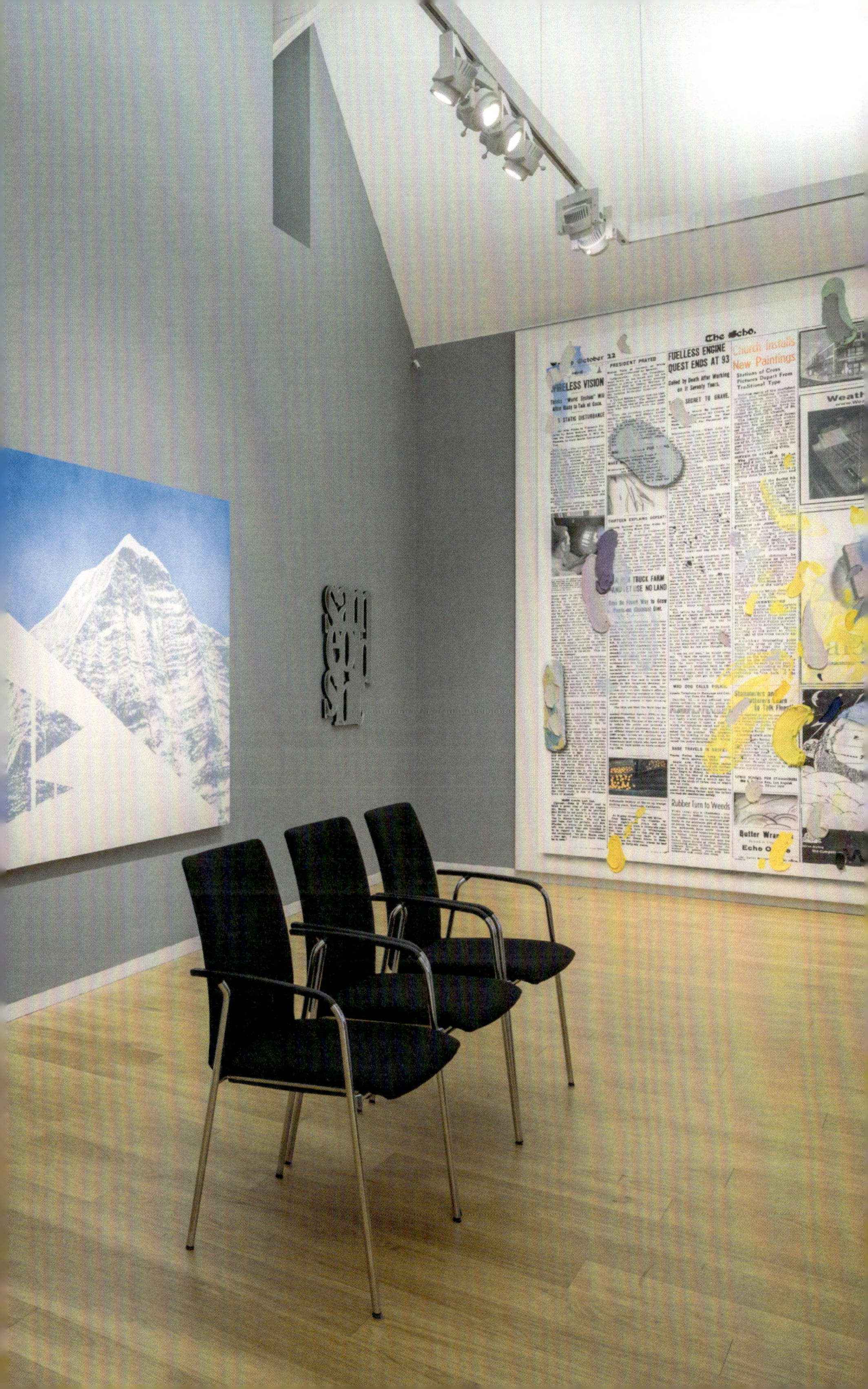

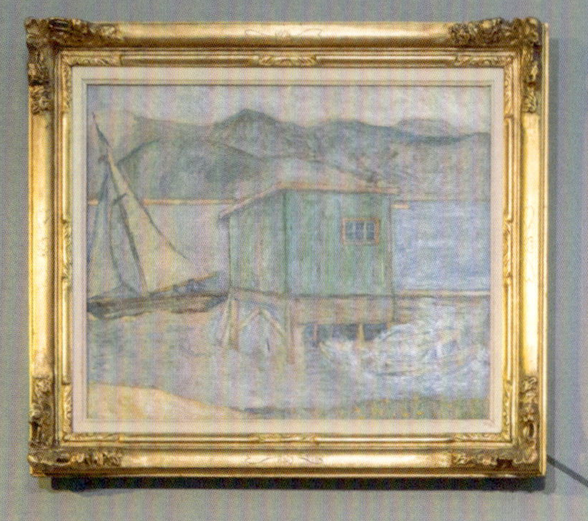

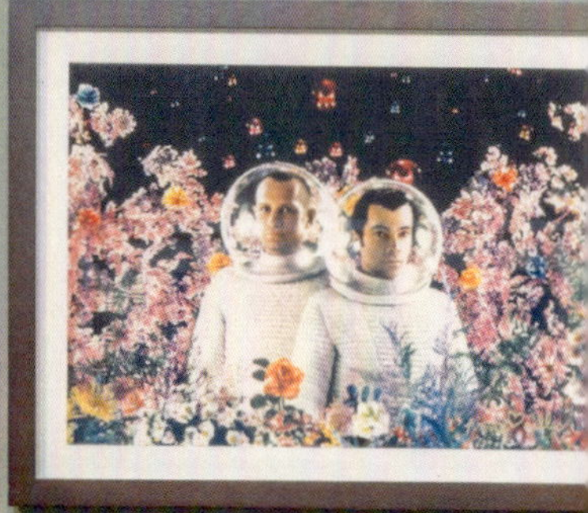

HOLLYWOOD

The Travel
BUREAU

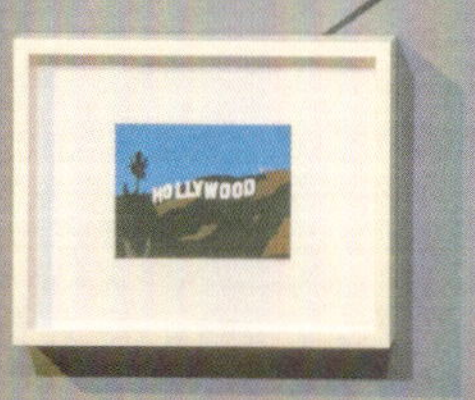

HOLLYWOOD

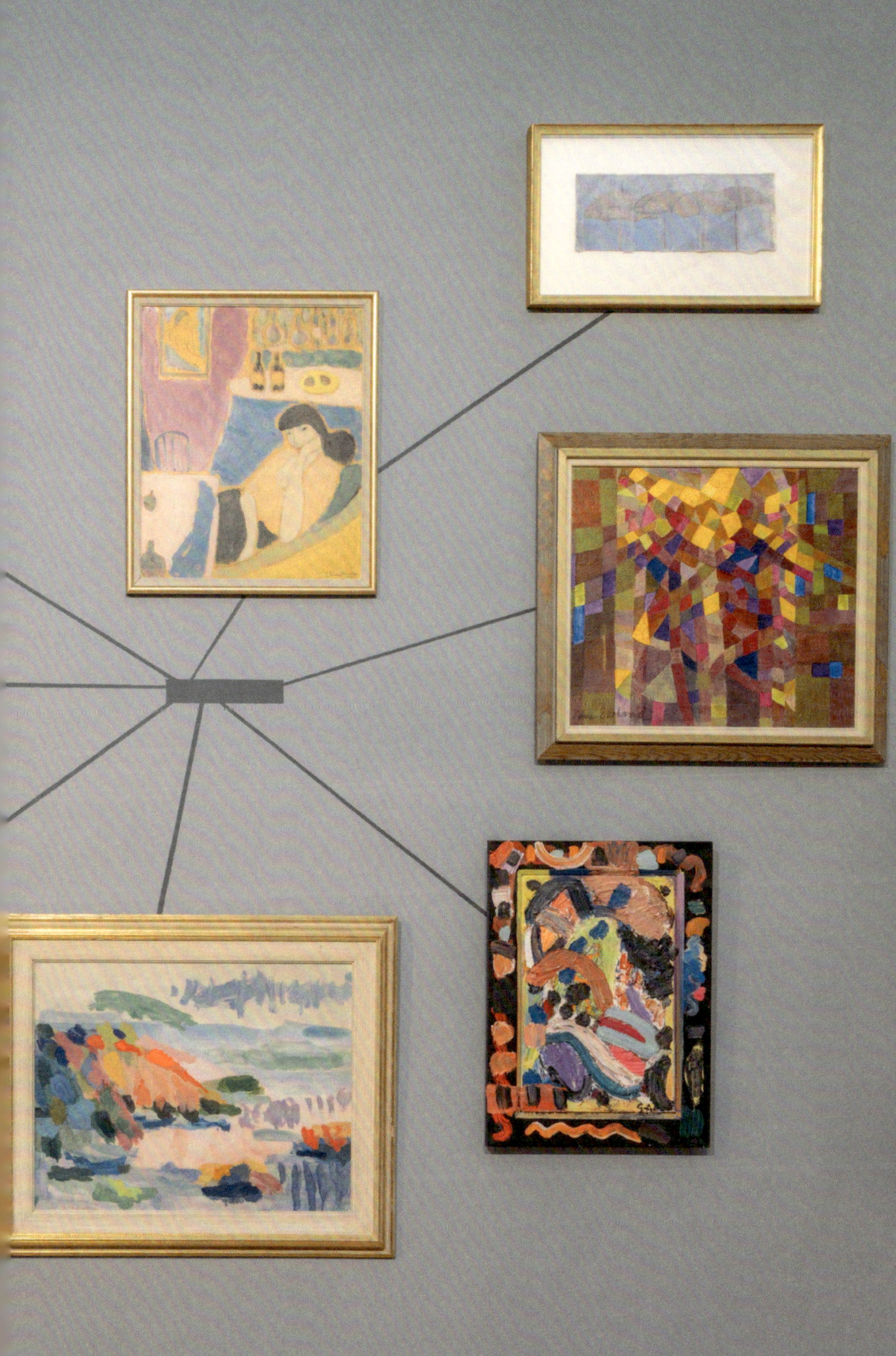

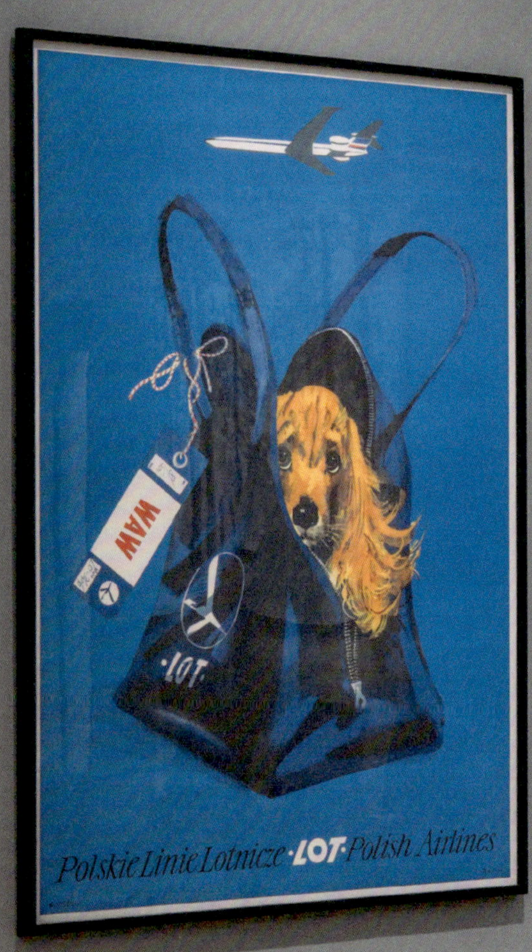
WAW
·LOT·
Polskie Linie Lotnicze ·LOT· Polish Airlines

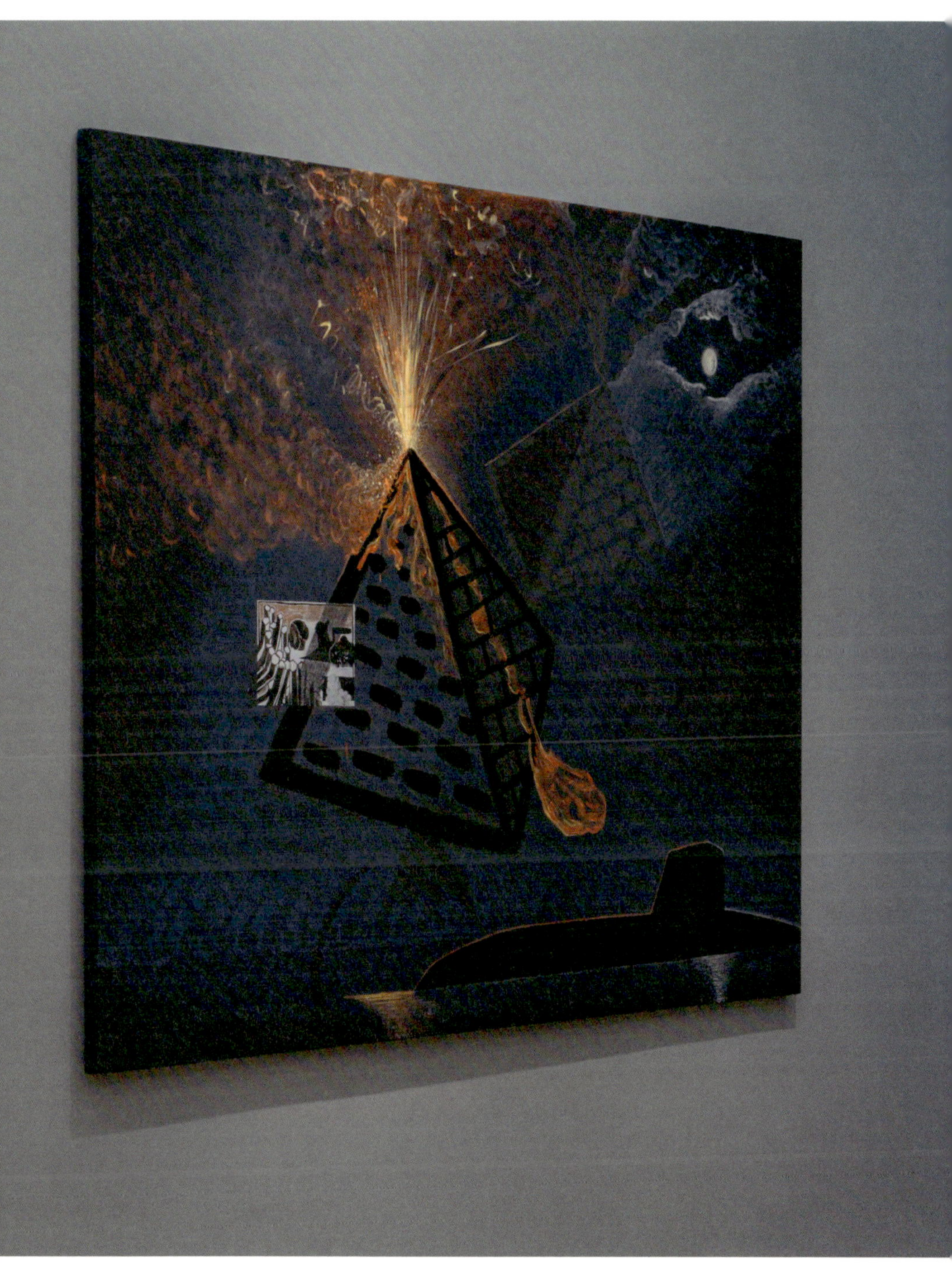

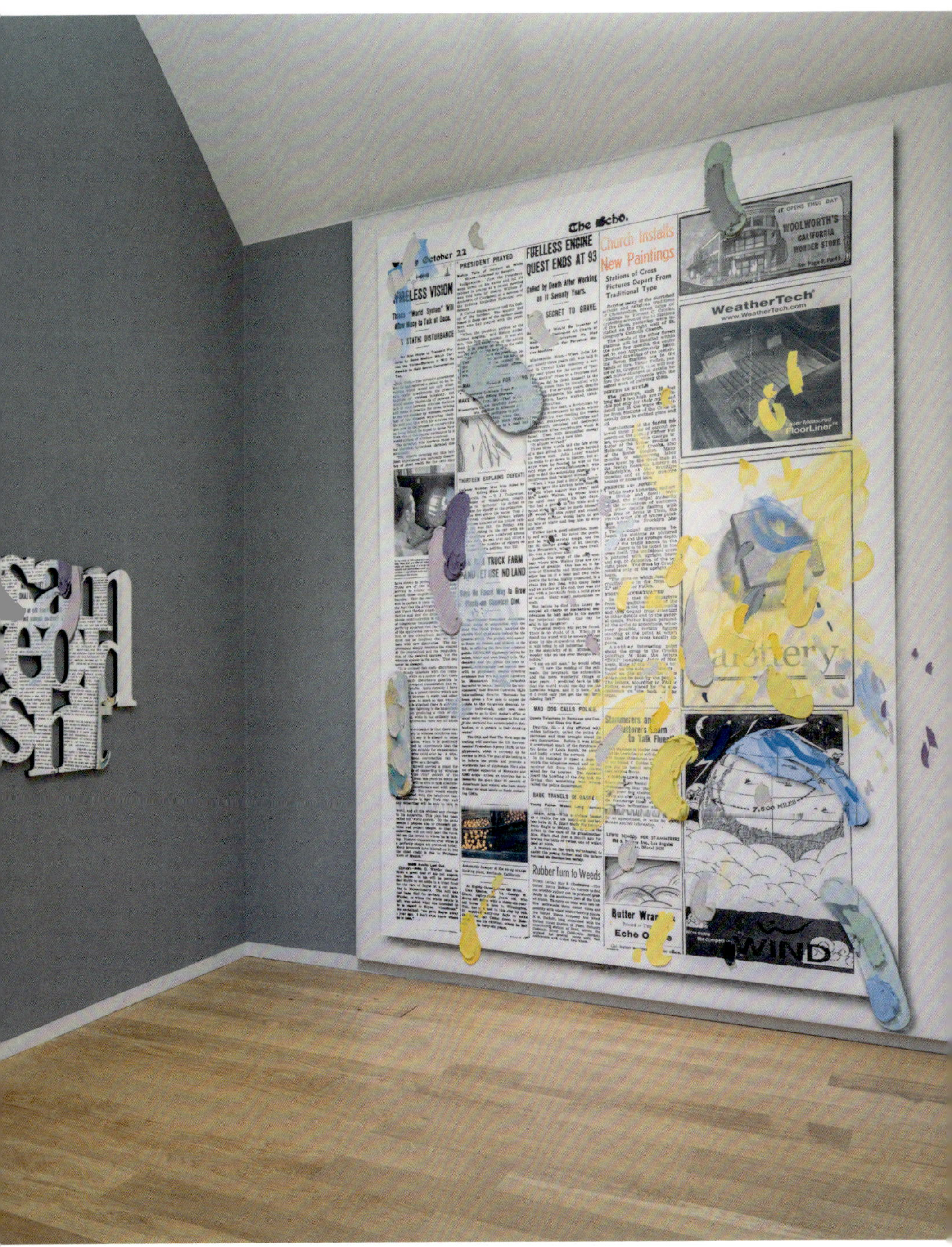

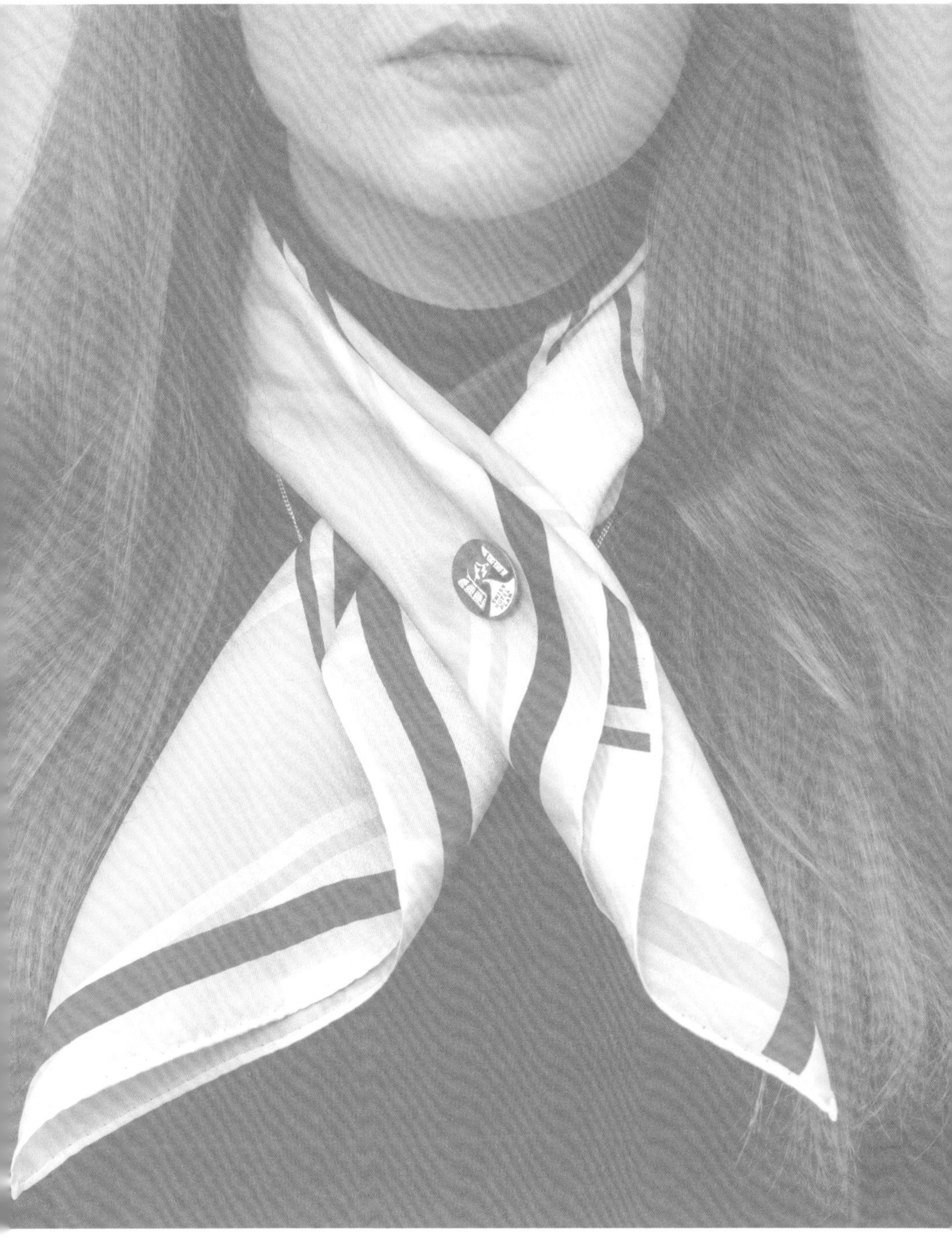

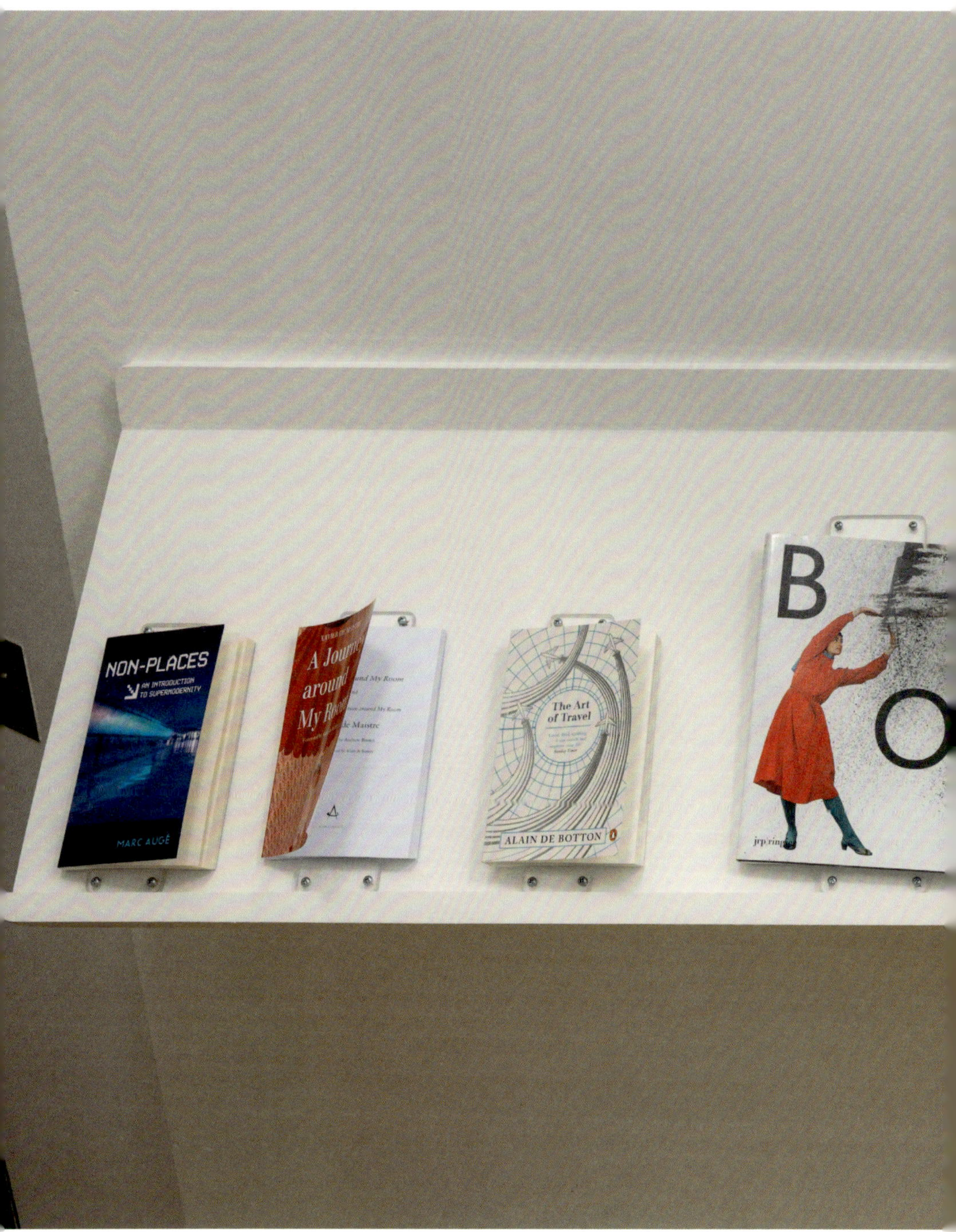
NON-PLACES
AN INTRODUCTION TO SUPERMODERNITY
MARC AUGÉ
A Journey around My Room
de Maistre
The Art of Travel
ALAIN DE BOTTON
jrp ringier

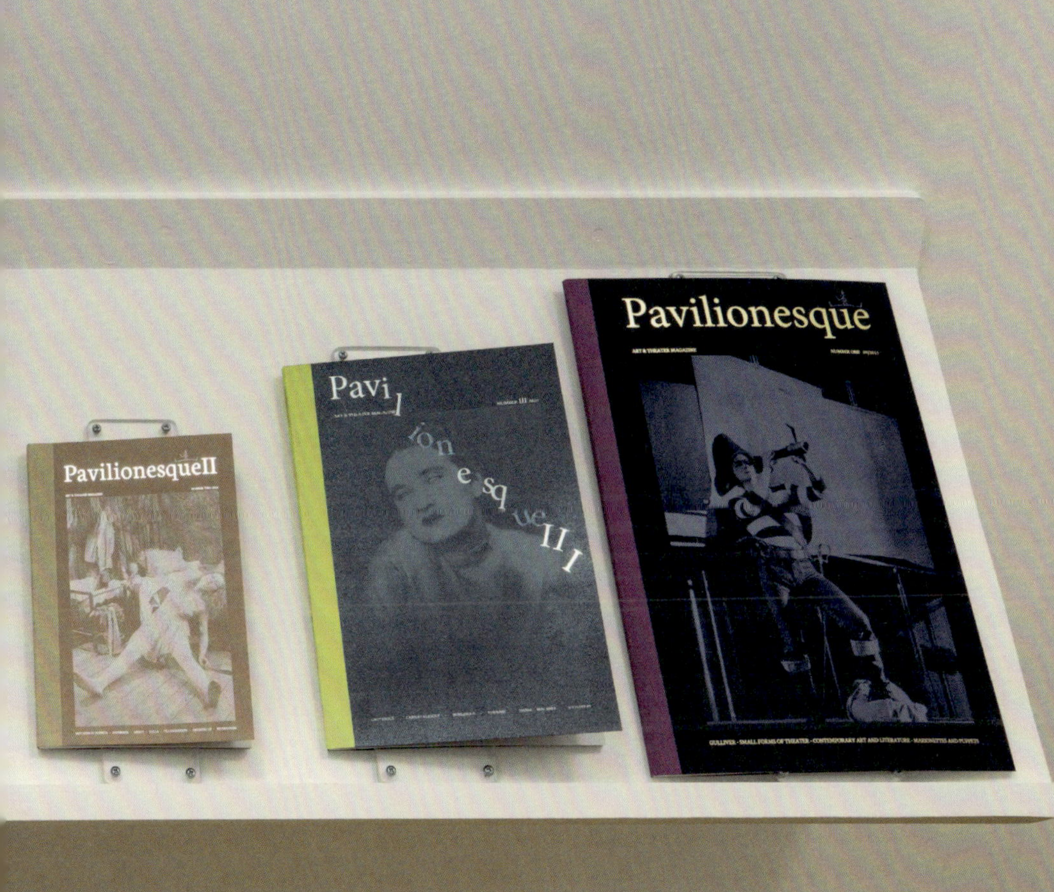

PavilionesqueII
Pavilionesque
Pavi
Pavilionesque
ART & THEATRE MAGAZINE
GULLIVER · SMALL FORMS OF THEATER · CONTEMPORARY ART AND LITERATURE · MARIONETTES AND PUPPETS

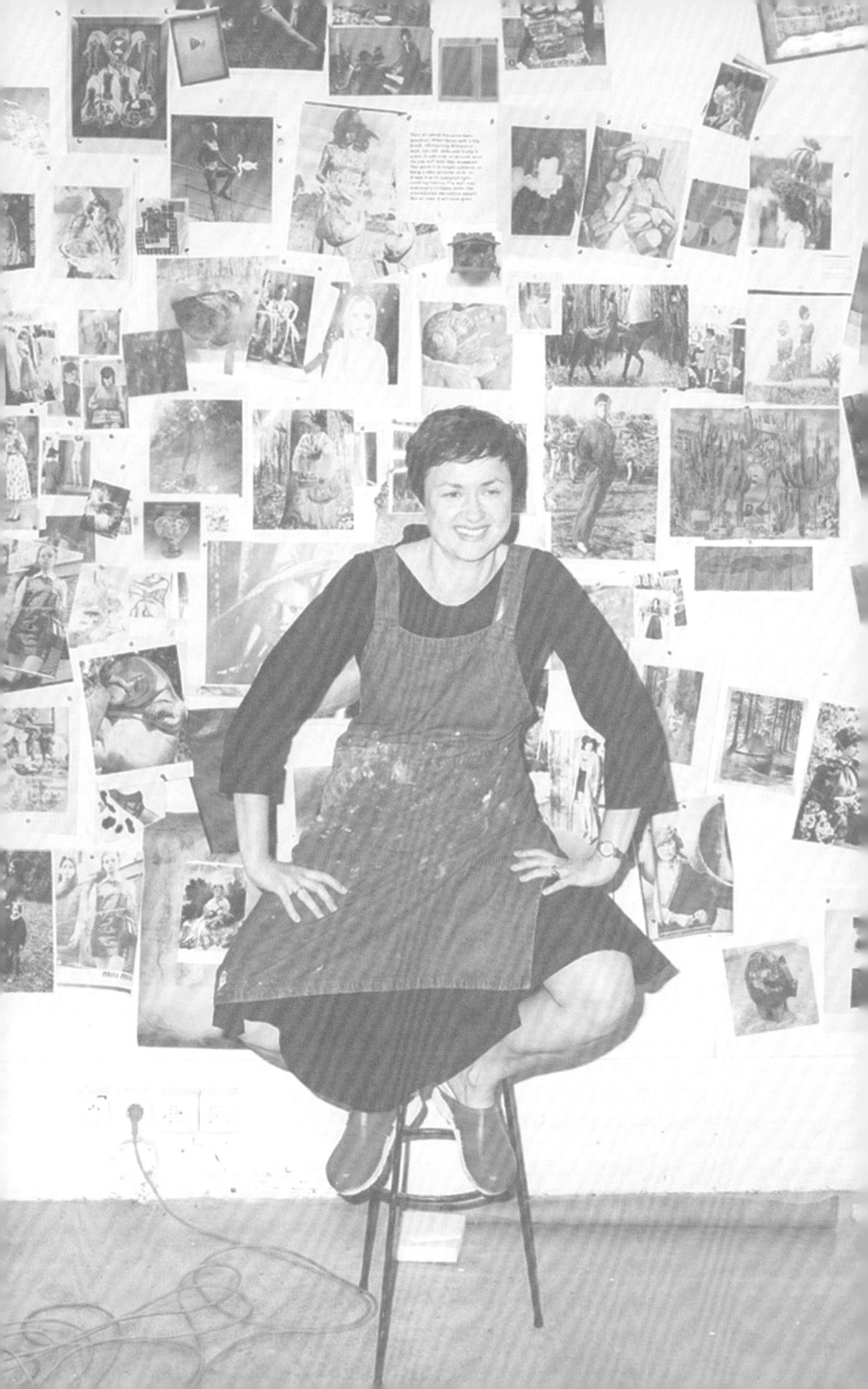

Painting as a Metaphor for Travel and Exhibitions as a Space of Experimentation

Paulina Olowska in conversation
with *Sabine Breitwieser*

SABINE BREITWIESER   Paulina, you are curating and creating the display for a selection of works from the Christen Sveaas Art Foundation as part of a series of exhibitions at the Whitechapel Gallery. Can you tell us how you've developed it?

PAULINA OLOWSKA   This will be the second presentation of works from the Christen Sveaas Art Foundation. The first was curated by Ida Ekblad, the third one will be curated by Hurvin Anderson and the fourth by Donna Huanca. The four of us have been given carte blanche in terms of how we can work with the collection. After looking at Ekblad's luscious and poetic presentation, 'This is the Night Mail', I was looking for a way to proceed with this large and varied selection of works. I decided to print images of the works I had preselected, which date from from 1913 to 2019, pin them to my studio wall and take a couple of days to contemplate them. It became apparent that throughout the images there were sets and scenes of different forms of landscape. In my works I usually like to find the special, unseen and unusual, but this time I was drawn to classical landscapes.

SB   I wouldn't expect that from you, but maybe you'll become one of those artists painting landscapes during the holidays! Let's discuss your interest in landscape further, but also your engagement with other artists.

41

Left: Paulina Olowska in her studio

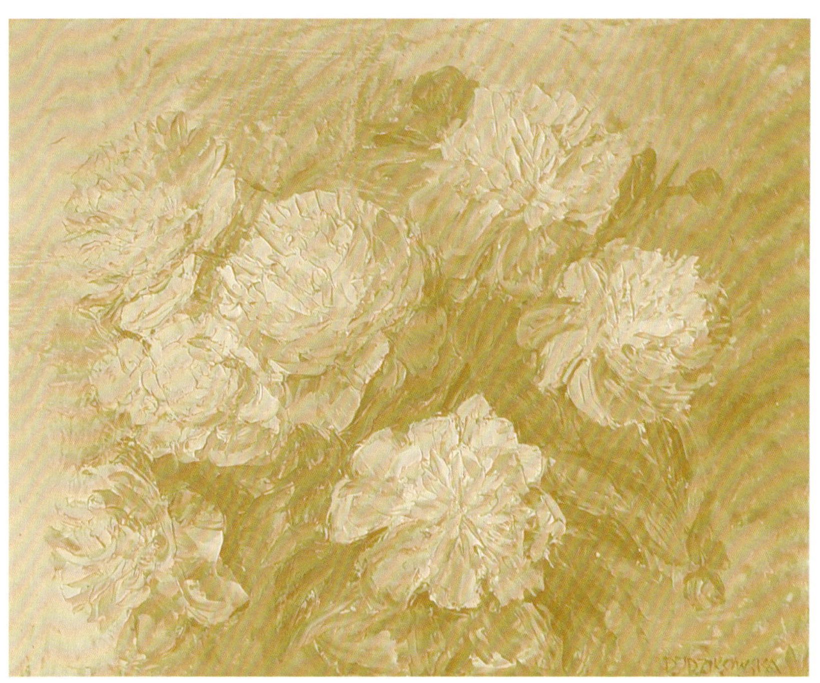

Danuta Idzikowska, *Peonies,* 1998, oil on carboard, 60 × 70 cm

<u>PO</u> I was surrounded by landscape painters growing up, and painting en plein air was a summer activity in my family. My grandmother Danuta loved the idea of going to the garden to draw. She had the idea that by drawing from nature and observing it closely, one understands it more intensely. Just like John Ruskin, she emphasised drawing as a basic anthropological skill.

Then I thought about how landscape relates to travel, the romantic vision of artists wanting to capture a place with the intensity of memory. What do places mean? What stories do they hide? And how do I work with landscape painting as a curator?

I have some experience working with exhibitions and curating other artists' works; usually my way of doing this was to create a form of theatricality in the space. For

example, in 2004 I presented a solo show, 'She Knew She
Had to Reject the Idea of a House as a Metaphor', at Kunstverein Braunschweig, where the whole show was a theatre
set with a narrative that audience members experienced
through the audio guide, and the lighting, walls and curtains
were all a part of the exhibition. In 2015, when hosting the
performance *The Mother: An Unsavoury Play in Two Acts
and an Epilogue* at Tate Modern, I used paintings from the
realism gallery to serve as the backdrop for a grotesque
theatre play. The actors treated the museum as they would a
stage. Thinking of the exhibition at the Whitechapel Gallery
and considering the institution's history of outstanding and
controversial displays, I decided to transform the exhibition
into a space from another time.

sb It's obvious that the role of an artist acting as a curator,
creating a mise-en-scène for other artists' works, is part of your
artistic practice and something you've been testing for a while.
In fact, one of the first times I came across your work was at the

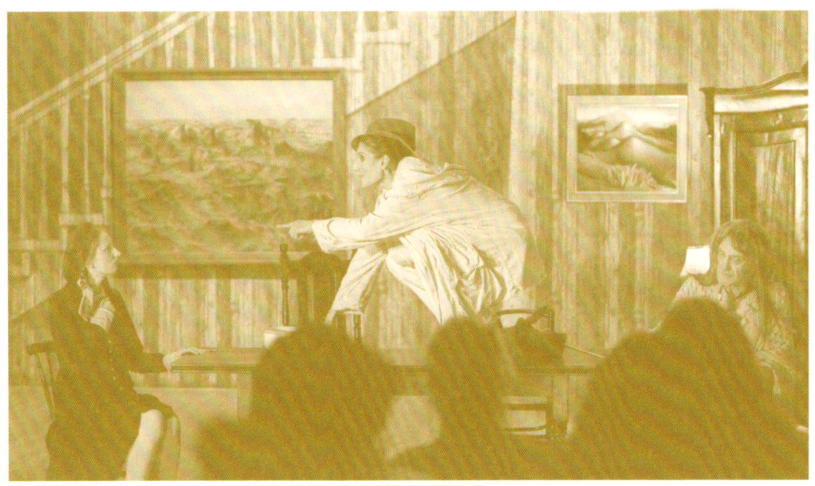

Paulina Olowska, *The Mother: An Unsavoury Play in
Two Acts and an Epilogue*, 2015, Tate Modern, London

Pinakothek der Moderne in Munich, where you selected only works by women artists for a collection display. Your interest in theatrically designed exhibitions reminds me of another Polish artist, Edward Krasinski, whose work you engaged with when you restaged *Farewell to Spring*, the 1968 ball Krasinski and his artist friends organised, where they invited the most influential figures of the Polish avant-garde as a challenge to the oppressive regime, which prohibited gatherings of more than three people. To create a mise-en-scène is one thing, but to select works from a collection is another. What does the selection process mean for you in terms of artistic creation?

PO Artworks have evocative force, they can become dialectical, narrative or controversial. But what happens when on top of their meaning there is a relationship to the space – like in Louise Lawler's photographs depicting other artists' works displayed in museums, storage spaces, auction houses and collectors' homes, where they gain a new meaning by her choice of framing. The works are placed in direct relationship to the space and a new dialogue is created. It's like a palimpsest of meaning. With artistic selection comes a parallel concept, which, in my case, was the stage set.

So I was thinking about how to frame a collection of landscapes. And then I read Marc Augé's *Non-Places: Introduction to an Anthropology of Supermodernity*, where he writes that 'travel constructs a fictional relationship between gaze and landscape.' That inspired me to create a stage set as a travel agency. The travel agency is an example of a waiting room, a space where you wait for an appointment. The room already lends itself to the idea of travel, with its social symbolism, so it is as though you are already travelling.

SB It's interesting that you're talking about real, physical travel, not about digital formats. Did you have a particular travel agent in mind?

<u>PO</u> Yes, the travel agency called Orbis in Warsaw, which closed twelve years ago. Their main office was by Constitution Square. Going there was like flying with a classy airline. The floors were carpeted, there were posters with amazing slogans on the walls and the travel agents were mostly women dressed as flight attendants. I lived around the corner, and I developed a strong bond with the women who worked there, they made me feel secure, and the way they talked about travel was masterful.

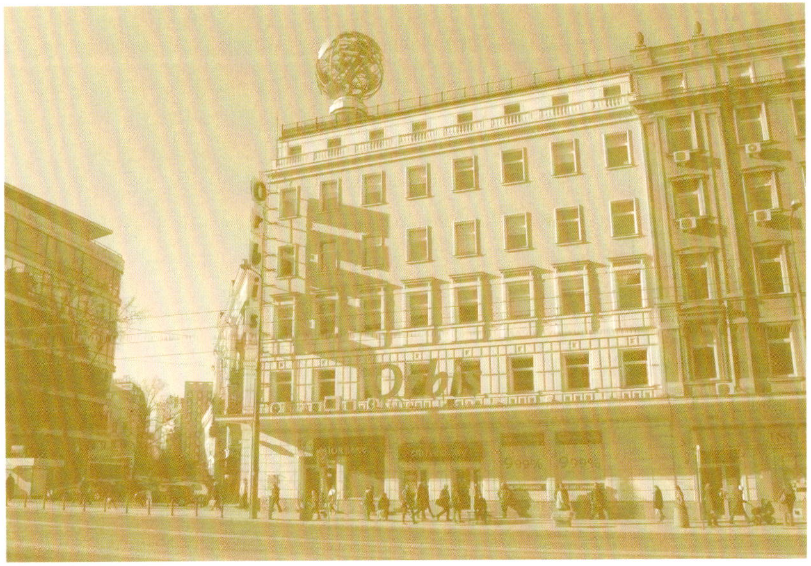

Orbis travel agency, Warsaw, Poland

<u>SB</u> The beautiful slide show you created as a reference for the look of the office is intriguing. Maybe this is, as you say, nostalgia for the aesthetics of 1950 and '60s offices or simply for an aeroplane ticket. Funnily enough, even though you are very tied to the physicality of travel, you used a digital format to communicate this aesthetic way to me, and you probably researched it digitally.

po Actually, I still have a lot of folders in my studio archives that are not digital, as even with the paintings from Christen Sveaas Art Foundation, the reproductions of the paintings were printed out.

This sense of longing might be passé, but it is also critical when recreated in the present. I do still see Orbis travel as a symbolic venue of socialist utopia. The Orbis logo was a globe, and there is still a large three-dimensional neon globe in Warsaw thanks to contemporary artists and other enthusiasts who rescued and illuminated it. The idea of unity and Earth as a sphere and the fullness of Earth fascinated me as a kid, and now, we don't think about it as a symbol of unity as much.

The difference that I see when I think about Orbis travel in relationship to Augé's ideas is that Orbis travel and similar travel agencies had a soul, they were this place of human exchange and relationships. Augé, as I understand it, is referencing a 'traveler's space [that] may thus be the archetype of non-place, meaning one of these in between spaces that provide homogenisation of needs and consumption....'

sb We see how you are driven by nostalgia and by spaces where specific relationships are formed. Would you share more about how you selected works from this large collection that was assembled by someone else?

po My attention was brought to a tiny painting from 1913 by Oluf Wold-Torne, a pastel-coloured Post-Impressionist painting of a seaside, which felt like the most symbolic, enchanting and undiscovered work. A work as a perfect symbol of an artist's personal memory. Another painting by Thore Heramb from 1958 and one by Arne Ekeland from 1965 caught my attention because of what they take from abstraction to landscape.

Berta Fischer's fluorescent acrylic glass sculpture for the wall, wow!

46

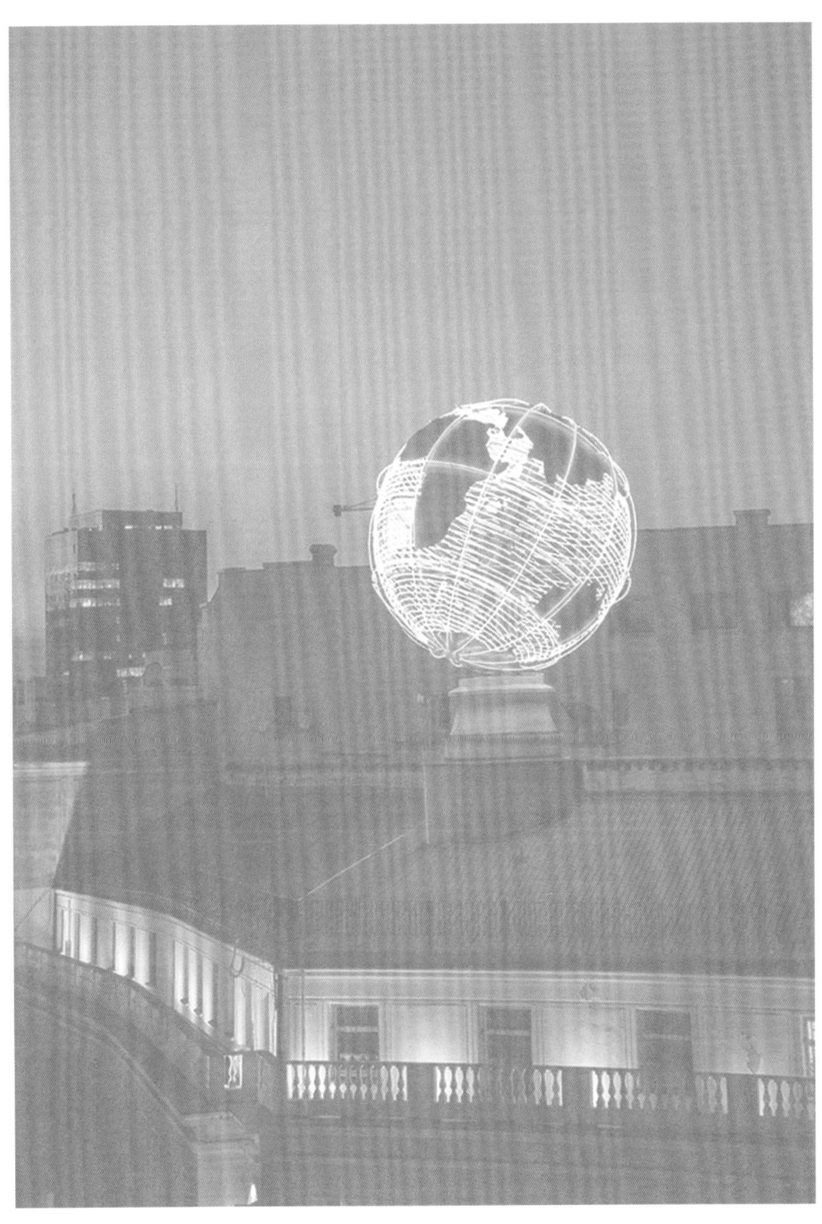

The Orbis globe on Jerozolimskie Avenue in Warsaw, Poland

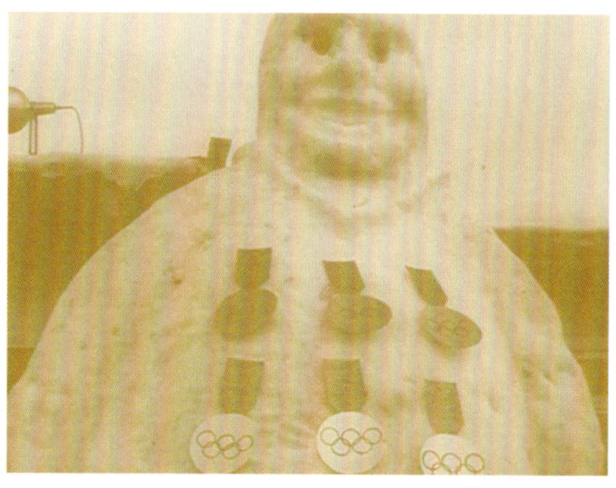

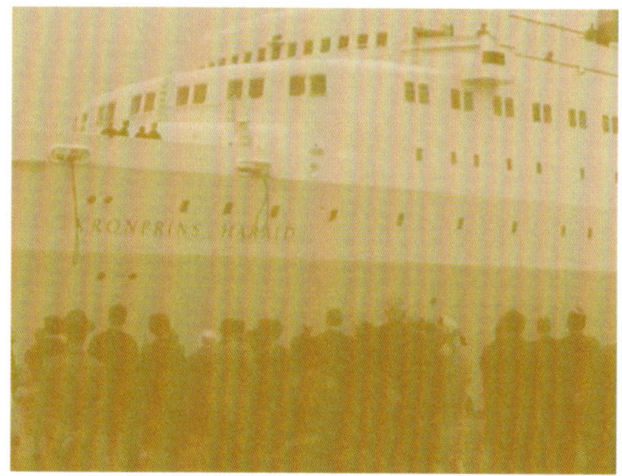

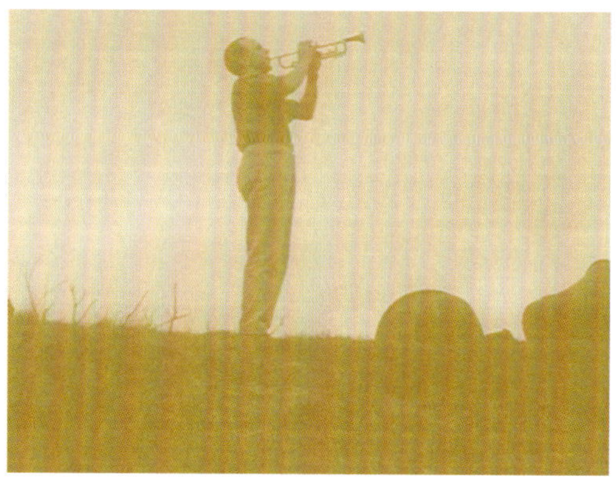

Paulina Olowska, *After Veiled Visions*, 2022
Film, music by Delia Gonzalez, archival material courtesy Filmparken og NRK,
Edited by Laura Grudniewska, 04' 54"

For me, there are three levels of reference to
travel – the first is the original posters from travel agencies
(from both Poland and Norway), the second is landscape
paintings (fantasy, real and plein air, notions of travel by
just imagining in works by Rodney Graham, Laura Owens,
Johannes Rian) and the third is works like those by Wold-
Torne, Heramb and Fischer, which have a more domestic
character and might have been found on the walls of offices
in the 1960s and '70s.

I am interested in the applied arts, so I was immedi-
ately drawn to Skuja Braden's painted ceramic vase *Ima
Woman*. Looking more closely at the aesthetics of the office,
it made sense to include works that are closer to abstraction, like Julia Rommel's painting *Ex-husband* or Charline
von Heyl's *Stationmaster* and Owens' *Untitled*, which all
play on the idea of post-object.

I have included works with a playful reference to
journeys, such as Brian Alfred's small collage *Hollywood* to
Pierre et Gilles' *Les Cosmonauts* and Marina Abramović's
The Hero, where the artist is sitting on a white stallion and
holding a flag.

sb How does the metaphor of a journey, or rather *the* journey, into
the collection unfold in your display?

po I included two videos in the show, one is called *After
Veiled Visions* from the Norwegian archives dating back
to around 1940 of scenes promoting Norwegian tourism.
It was then edited by Laura Grudniewska with music by
Delia Gonzalez. I'm juxtaposing this video with the work
Fra Skogen (From the Forest) by Norwegian artist Jakob
Weidemann. The second video is a reedited video titled
Univermag GUM *(Episode Airport)* from 2018 that I shot in
Minsk, Belarus, in public places such as the theatre, the GUM
department store and the airport, set to music by Halina
Zolotuho. This is displayed alongside my painting from the
Christen Sveaas Art Foundation titled *Window Display* GUM,

after the department stores in Minsk and Moscow. Department stores of that era, like Minsk airport, have a ghostly appearance of the socialist take on such locations.

SB What about the work chosen for the cover of the catalogue?

PO I admire Hurvin Anderson's work. His collage *Blue and Gold Umbrella* is on the cover of the catalogue as an announcement for 'The Travel Bureau'. I knew Anderson's larger landscape paintings but this intimate metallic work on paper really touched me. It might look very English, but then I learned from the artist that it was a part of his undergraduate degree show in 1994 and was based on Ethiopian prayer umbrellas, which I liked because it gives an image of other symbols and places.

SB Your mise-en-scène for travelling through the collection makes me think about one of your most famous works, *Nova Popularna*. In this bar that you created with Lucy McKenzie in 2003 in Warsaw, you also performed and hosted a series of events. Can we expect a programme of special events as part of this exhibition?

PO Yes, the exhibition relates to the idea of the Gesamtkunstwerk. *Nova Popularna* was a bar, meeting place and salon organised by Foksal Gallery foundation that I ran together with McKenzie. Certainly, back then Warsaw as a city was very raw so our visionary salon was quite utopian, but we were also operating as an illegal bar. 'The Travel Bureau' is more a metaphor for painting as travel by itself.

SB Real travel may be inspiring, but it can also be quite uncomfortable, both physically and mentally. I am wondering if your travel has a beginning and an end, or how the itinerary of your travel, the travel you invite the audience to undertake, is organised. What will visitors encounter?

PO I'm trying to conceive of this exhibition as being on the borderline of the performative, so viewers will have a feeling that something can be performative, but actually, that will be only the experience of the viewers of the works. There will be a feeling that something can happen, from moment to moment. That somebody might come.

SB How do you feel about the reversed role in general with this project? You are an artist who, for this project, is selecting works and curating an exhibition, in comparison to someone like me, a curator, selecting works and organising a show, for instance with your works? Do you think my job is obsolete and you as an artist can do much better when making choices and designing exhibitions?

PO That's an interesting way to put it. I really enjoy curating and I enjoy you as a curator. How do you feel when artists curate exhibitions?

SB In my role as director of the Generali Foundation, once a year, I invited artists (who had often never done something like that before) to curate a thematic exhibition. This series of projects was challenging in many ways, but we always got a completely fresh perspective on topics and artists as well as beautiful, experimental displays. Do you know if Iwona Blazwick, the director of Whitechapel Gallery, who invited you – we could also say, she 'curated' you – has specific expectations for your project? I wonder whether there is an overlapping of what people see in your work, what they get from your work, whether this would make us look at the collection as if through a certain foil.

PO Reading Alain de Botton's *The Art of Travel*, I came across a text by Xavier de Maistre titled *A Journey Around My Room* in which a young officer, upon finding himself locked in his room for six weeks, uses his imagination to travel around the chamber, using the various objects it contains. I like to think of paintings as objects through which you imagine a place and what can happen when you reach it.

<u>SB</u> I guess the exhibition also presents the opportunity to create your own context, how you would like to see your work situated. In this instance, you revisit forgotten artists whose work you feel strongly about, but at the same time, you also create a context for other artists. As a curator, I would reach out to an artist and involve them in the project. As an artist in the role of a curator, will you reach out to the artists and authors who produced the artworks you select?

<u>PO</u> The method of curating in 'The Travel Bureau' is irrational. What it means is hard to describe clearly in language. It's something that many artists build and the outcome is unpredictable.

I'll conclude with an English poet William Wordsworth's words describing the poet's joy while taking a morning walk after a rainy night:

I was a Traveller then upon the moor;
I saw the hare that raced about with joy;
I heard the woods and distant waters roar;
Or heard them not, as happy as a boy:
The pleasant season did my heart employ:
My old remembrances went from me wholly;
And all the ways of men, so vain and melancholy.[1]

---

1 William Wordsworth, 'Resolution and Independence', 1802, https://www.poetryfoundation.org/poems/45545/resolution-and-independence

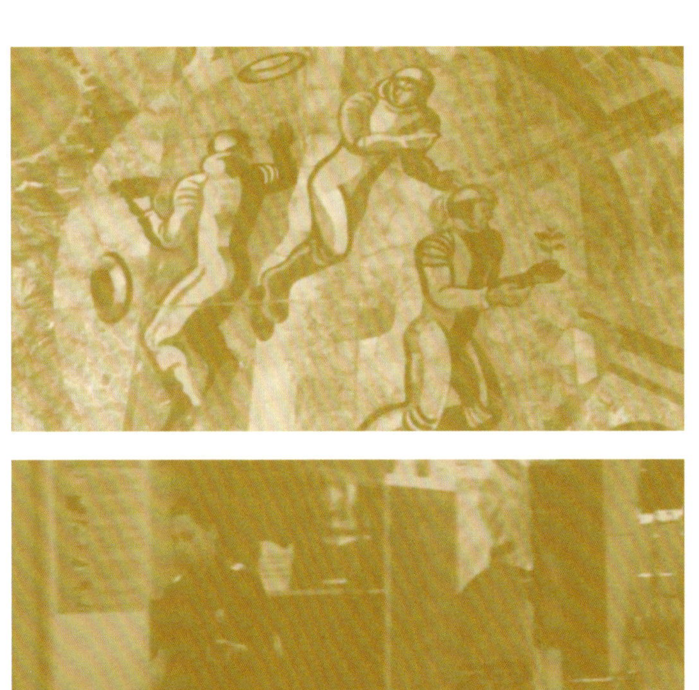

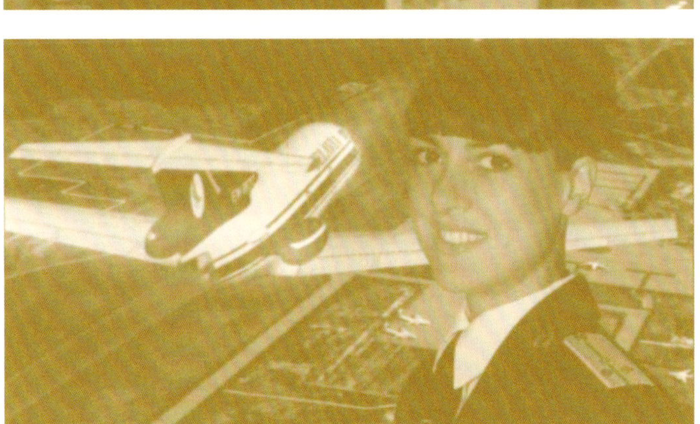

Paulina Olowska, *Univermag G.U.M. (Episode Airport)*, 2018
Film, 1' 51"

53

Marina Abramović

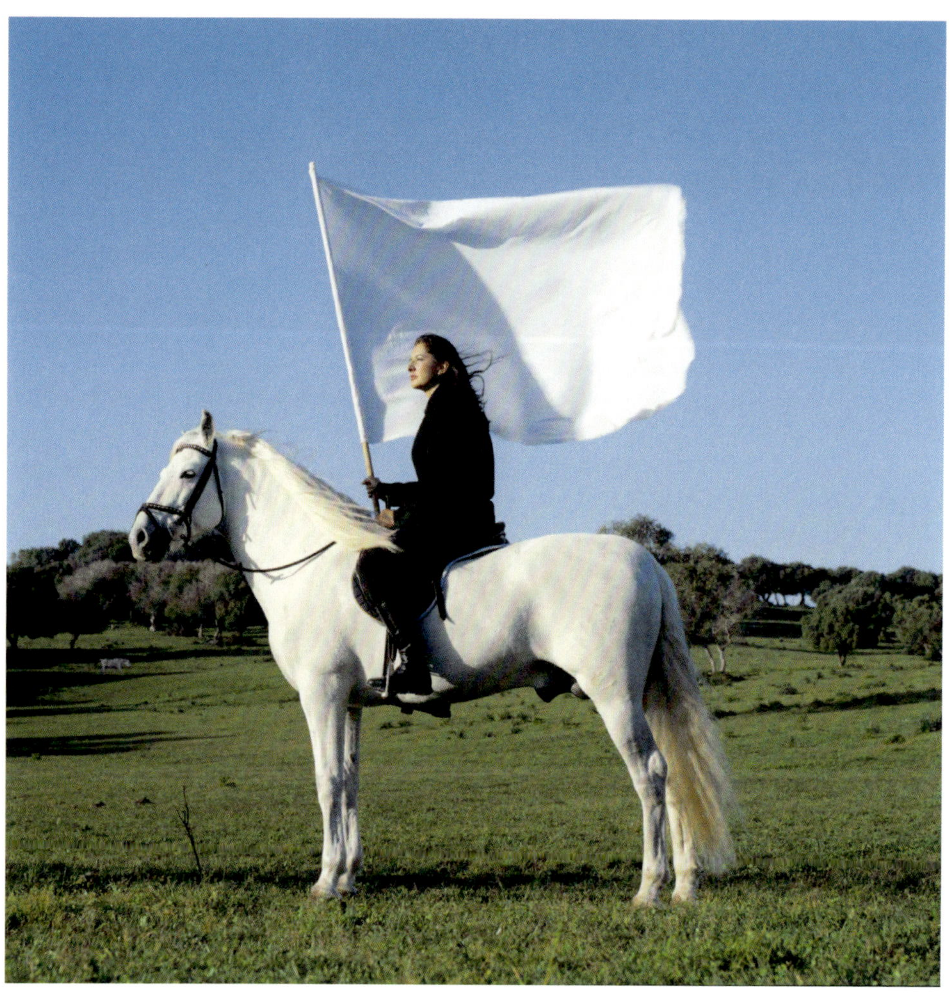

Marina Abramović (1946 Serbia) is famous for her groundbreaking performance work in the 1970s, characterised by a willingness to expose her own body to extreme physical exertion to produce certain mental states. Abramović's work tests the limits of the human body for pain, combined with extreme endurance, inner intensity and physical commitment. Often, there is also a desire to involve and engage the spectators in the work, as part of the artist's complex and nuanced relationship to the audience: *'In real life, you just work for the ordinary self, but in the front of audience you become the superself. That's a completely different thing.'* IAK

Marina Abramović, *The Hero*, 2001
Colour photograph, 123 × 123 × 7.62 cm

Brian Alfred

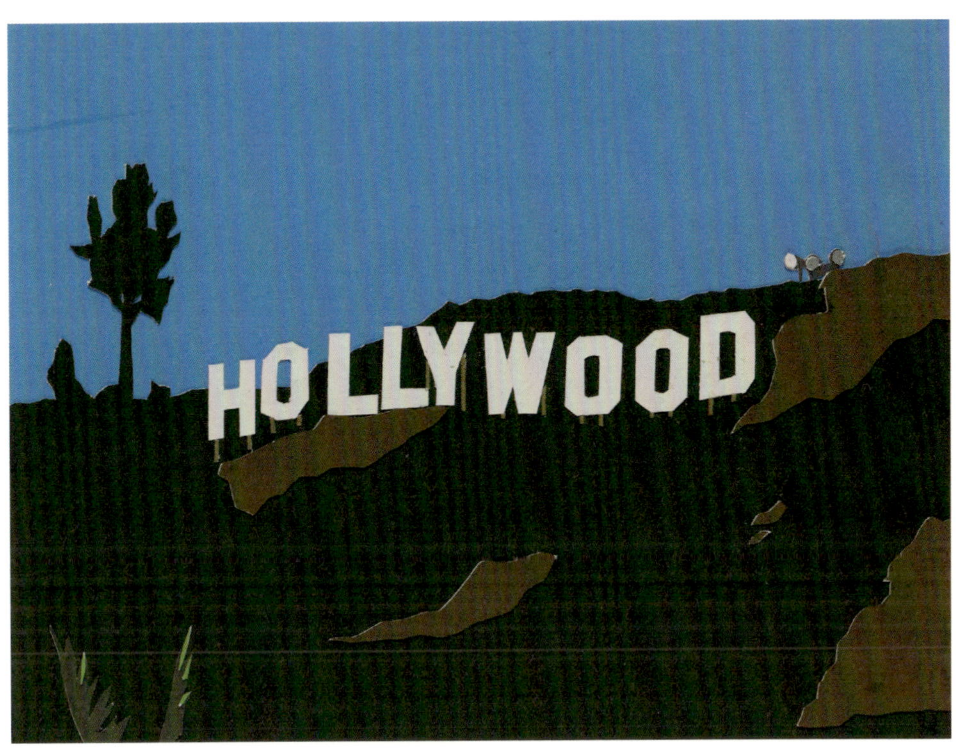

Brian Alfred (1974 USA) works across a range of mediums from painting and collage to digital animation and music. The artist explores a range of subject matters in his work, from architecture and technology to notions of romantic heroism. His two-dimensional works tend to be flattened and depopulated with colourful patterns that are often sourced from found imagery in newspapers, television and the internet. Alfred explores the effects that public and widely accessible imagery has on individual perceptions of reality. The artist says of his paintings, *'I like that they look relatively flat from afar, but there's a reward when you get up close.'* TM

Brian Alfred, *Hollywood*, 2005
Collage on paper, 25.4 × 31.8 cm

Hurvin Anderson

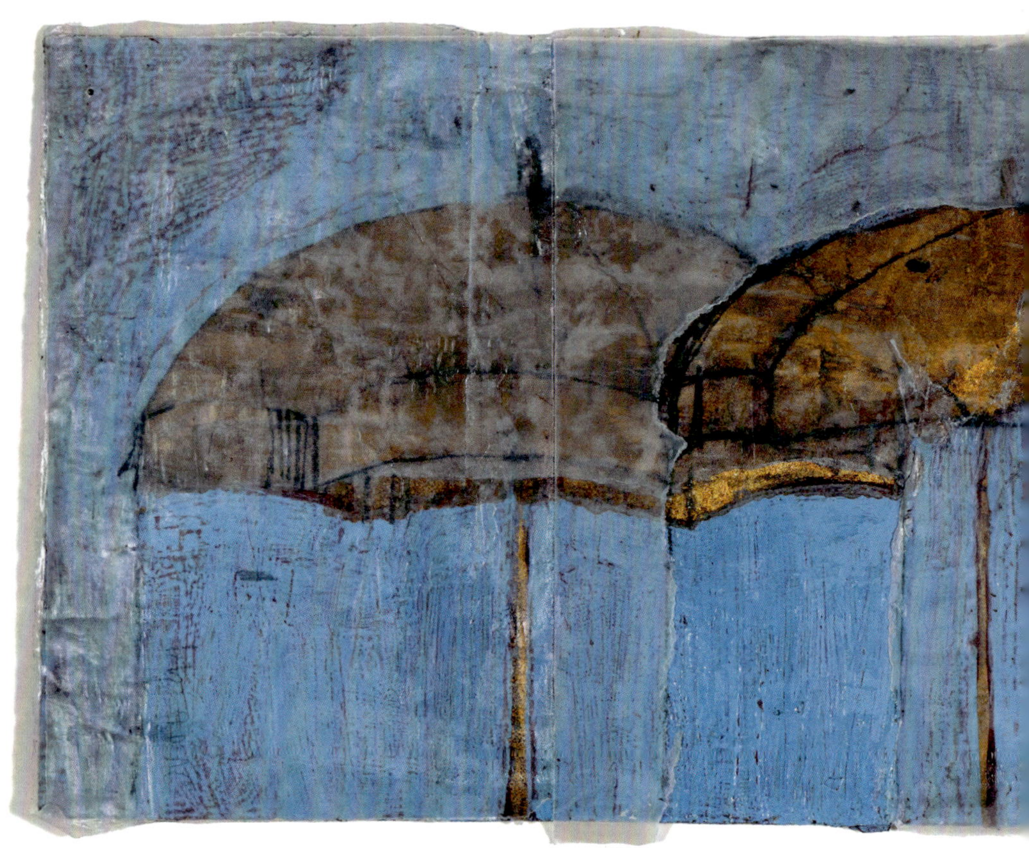

Hurvin Anderson (1965 United Kingdom) was born in Birmingham to parents of Jamaican descent and studied in London at the Wimbledon College of Arts and the Royal College of Art. His vivid paintings are embedded with the cultural and social history of his origins and explore notions of belonging and memory that draw on the complexity of the diasporic experience. Although Anderson's works are largely representational, he typically disrupts their legibility with abstract patterns, setting up contradictions and juxtapositions that evoke the indeterminacy of being between cultures. For the artist, painting is a *'dialogue between these two territories – trying to get these two places to meet'*. TM

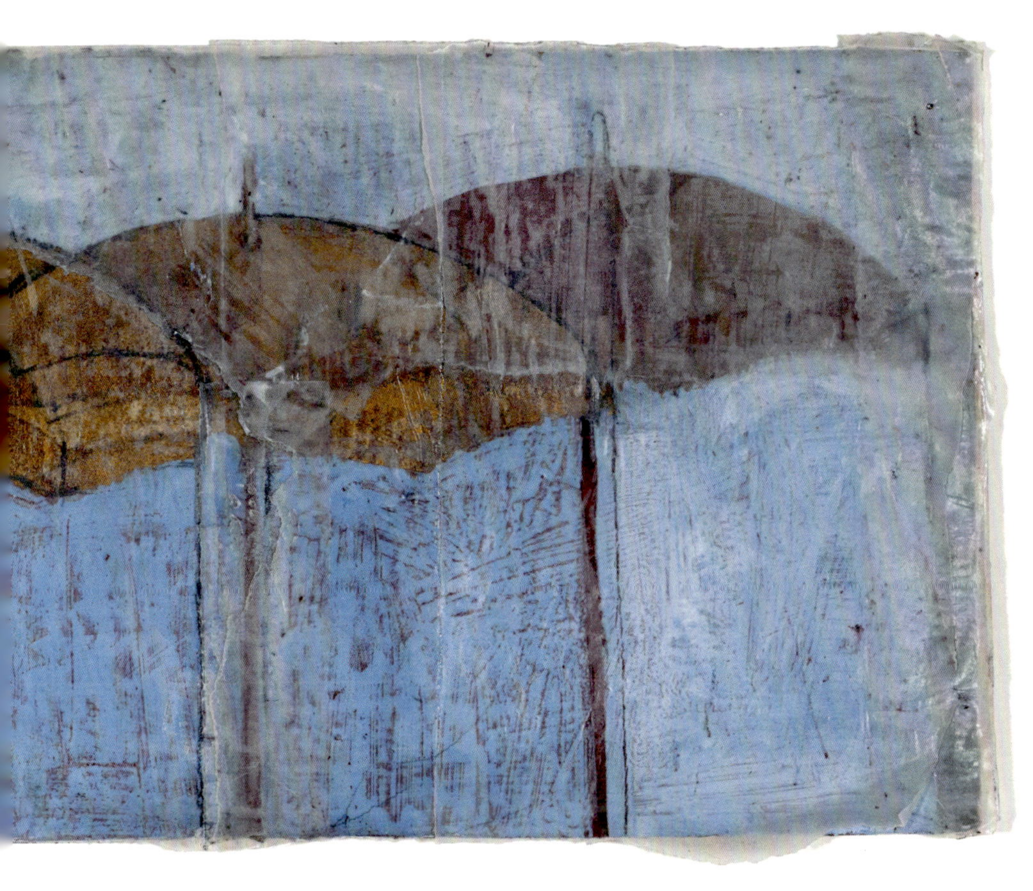

Hurvin Anderson, *Blue and Gold Umbrella*, 1994
Pencil, oil, metallic paint, glassine and newspaper collage on paper, 14.8 × 40 cm

Gillian Ayres

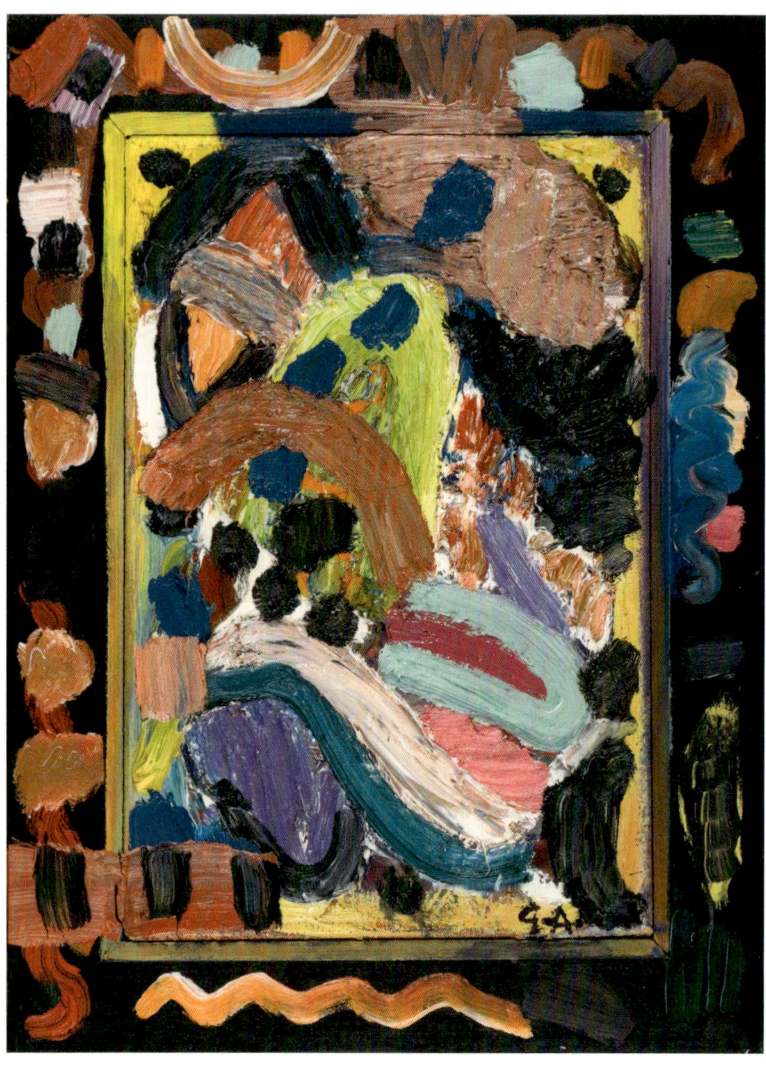

Gillian Ayres (1930–2018 ᴜᴋ) is renowned for her large, vividly coloured abstract paintings and prints. She was among the first British painters to be influenced by Abstract Expressionism and gained critical attention when her paintings were included in the 1960 exhibition 'Situation' at the Royal Society of British Artists, in which she was the only woman to exhibit, and in the exhibition 'British Painting in the 60s' at the Whitechapel Gallery in 1963. Ayres referred to visual language as something separate from verbal language, remarking, *'to me, painting is a visual thing, and that's it. People like to understand, and I wish they wouldn't! I wish they'd just look.'* ɢs

Gillian Ayres, *Hark Hark the Lark*, 1984–1990
Oil on canvas, 46 × 31 cm

Monica Bonvicini

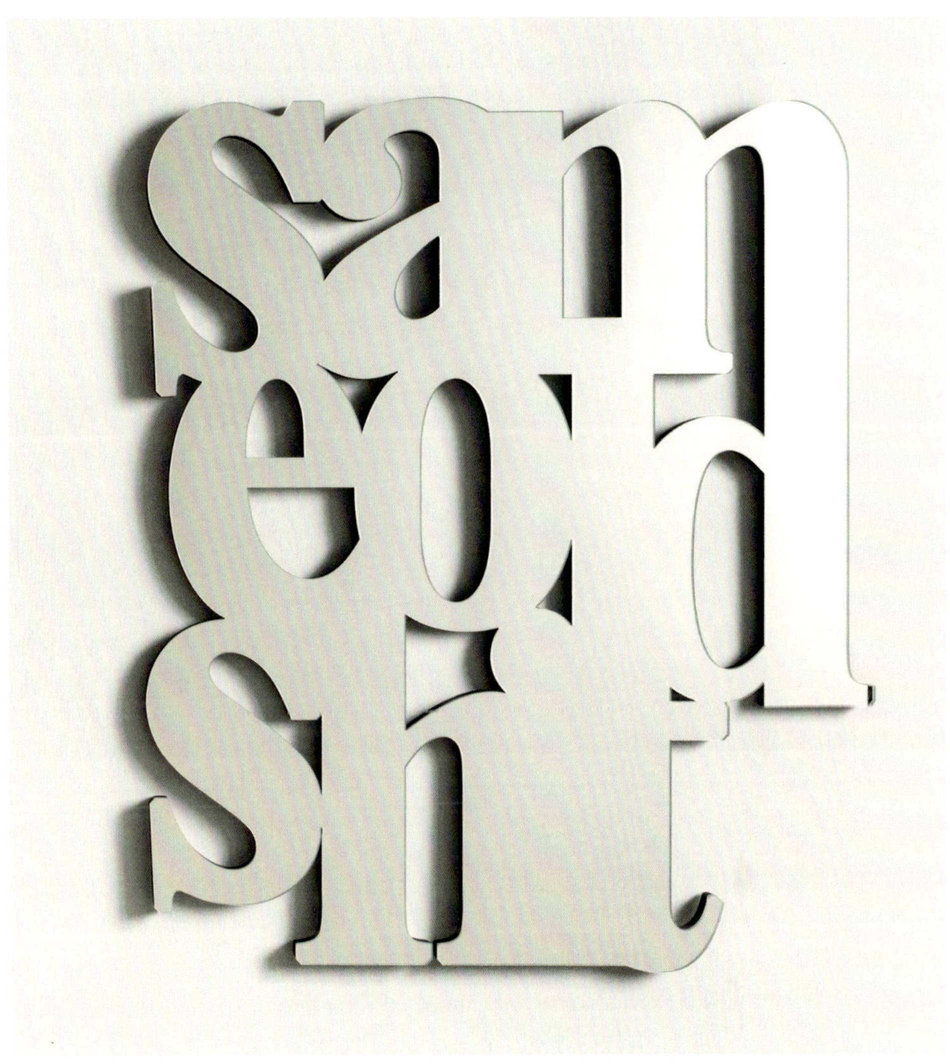

Monica Bonvicini's (1965 Italy) artistic practice spans sculpture, installation, film, performance and writing. She began exhibiting her work internationally in the early 1990s following her graduation from the Universität der Künste, Berlin and from the California Institute of the Arts. Exploring the relationship between architecture, control, surveillance and power, Bonvicini's art is often site-specific and makes critical connections between the roles of spectator and creator. For Bonvicini, humour and language are tools to deconstruct notions of gender within constructed spaces and male-dominated environments. She states, *'Art has always been a social mirror. I expect that from art.'* TM

Monica Bonvicini, *Same Old Shit*, 2018
Mirror, MDF, 83.8 × 74.3 × 2.5 cm

Rosson Crow

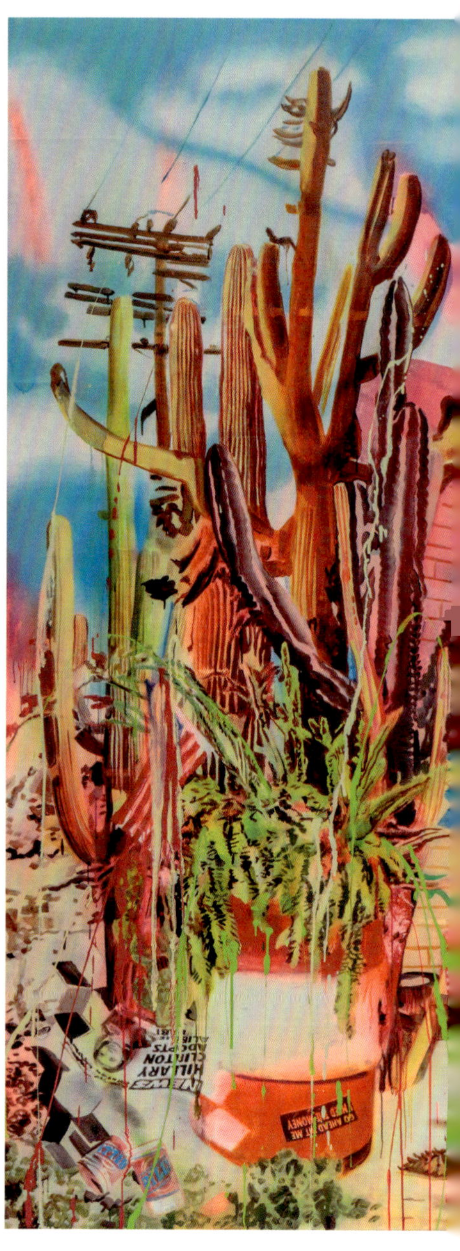

Rosson Crow (1982 USA) lives and works in Los Angeles, USA. The surfaces of her large-scale paintings are densely layered with acrylic, spray paint, Xeroxed photo transfers, oil and enamel and juxtapose images, artefacts and icons from various periods in order to explore how historic events are viewed differently across time. In a recent body of work, Crow takes the desert landscape as a point of departure, painting the rubbish, relics and plant life populating the sandy floor. She comments, *'I want the viewer to be overwhelmed. I want the space to feel like it is caving in on the viewer and that they are entering the world of my paintings. I don't want them to be subtle.'* GS

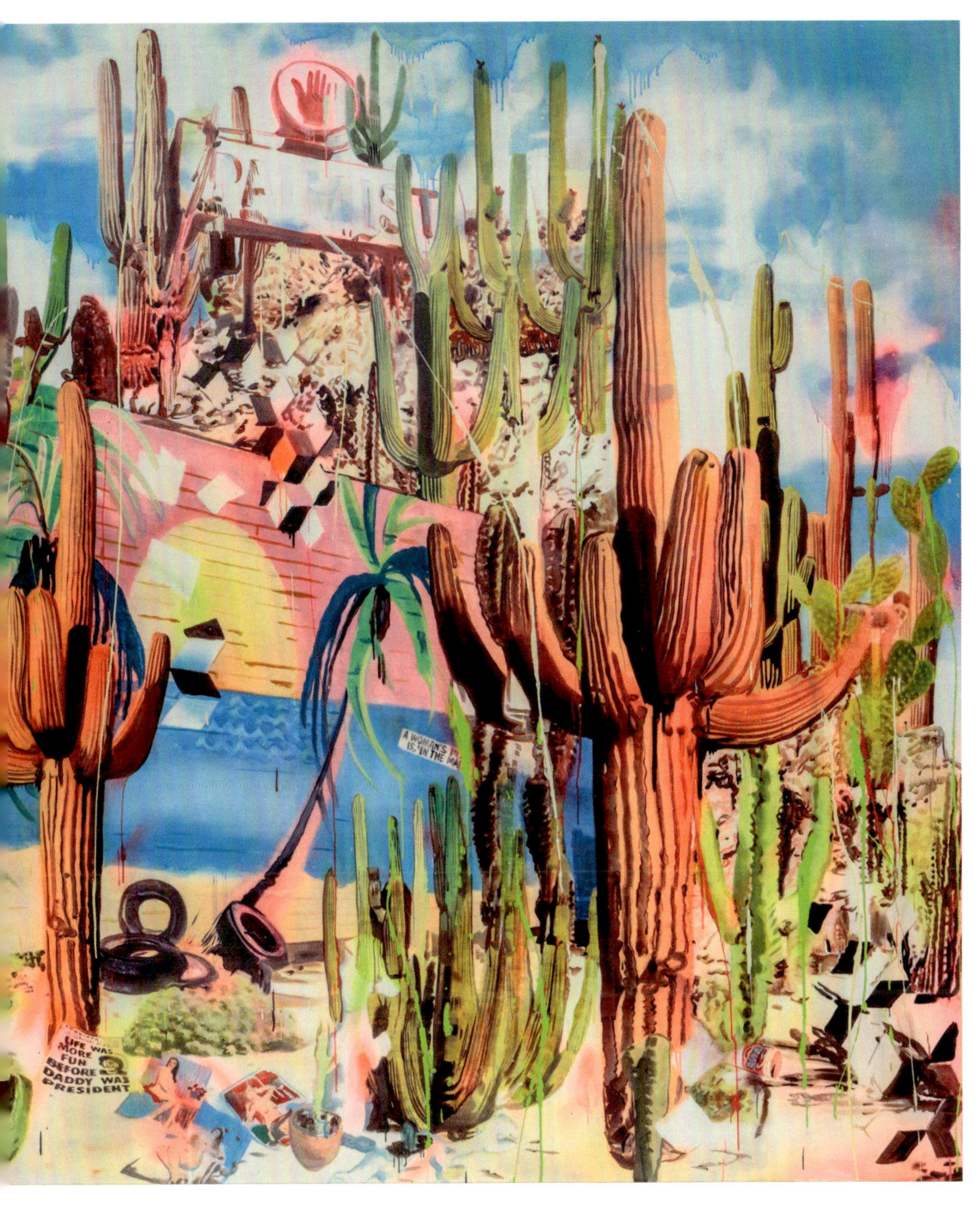

Rosson Crow, *Relics of the Truth Tellers*, 2017
Acrylic, spray paint, photo transfer, oil and enamel on canvas, 274 × 365.8 cm

Ida Ekblad

Ida Ekblad (1980, Norway) lives and works in Oslo, Norway. Her practice incorporates painting, sculpture, performance, filmmaking and poetry. The forms and gestures found in her work are inspired by a variety of sources that range from art historical movements such as CoBrA, Situationism and Abstract Expressionism to the pop culture aesthetic of graffiti or cartoons. The energetic movement of her compositions, her bold application of colour and the attentive use of found materials generate a potent vibrancy and dynamic spontaneity. *'Whatever sense I find,'* she says, *'is primarily an aesthetic sense. In painting, sculpture, and via material twists and turns, I am striving to make a personal and decent pattern of what happens to come my way.'* CS

Ida Ekblad, *The Proofreader*, 2017
Lacquer and acrylic on cotton with ink, puff and plastisol on cotton, 180 × 140 cm

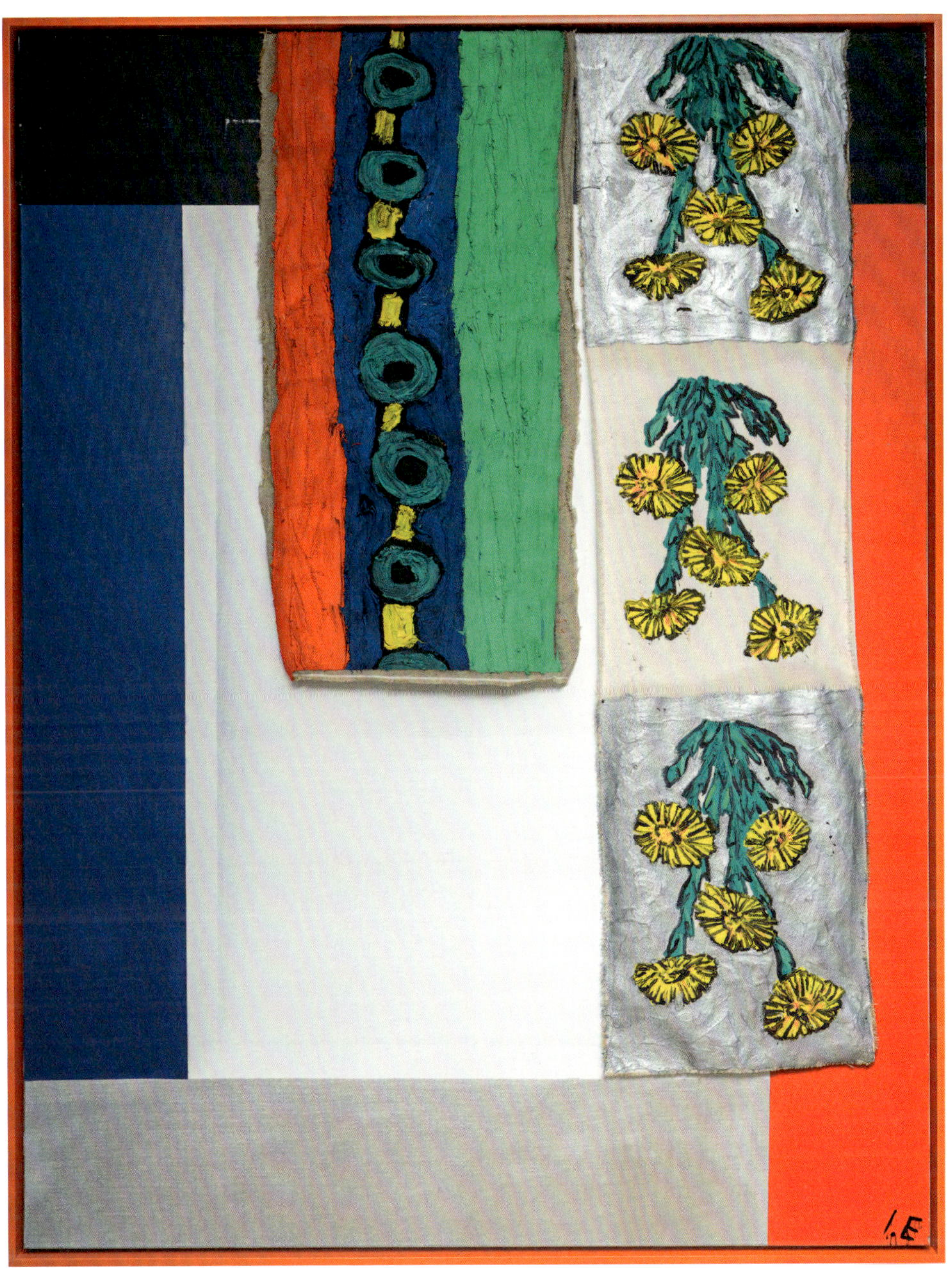

Arne Ekeland

Arne Ekeland (1908–1994 Norway) was a leading figure in twentieth-century Norwegian art. His influences range from Italian Renaissance art to Cubism, Expressionism and Byzantine art. Ekeland was a declared communist from a working-class background, and a large part of his oeuvre can be seen as an attempt to create a Marxist iconography. He painted scenes of class struggle, revolution and repression but also beauty, sexuality and nature. Because of his convictions he was not always in favour with the political establishment, who turned down his proposals to adorn the Oslo City Hall and Norwegian Parliament building on the basis that their content was too divisive. He has said: '*Art shouldn't be at grassroots level because art should bring us out of the ordinary and away from everyday life.*' AGK

Arne Ekeland, *Møte i porten* (Meeting at the Gate), 1965 Oil on canvas, 51 × 58.5 cm

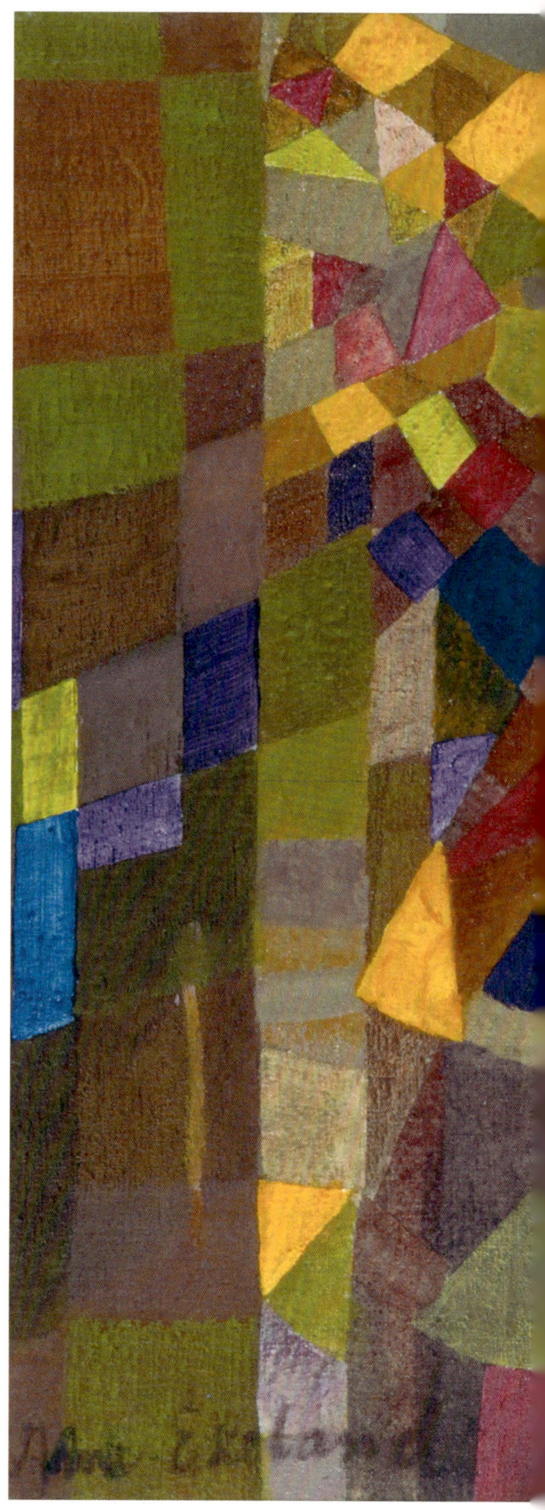

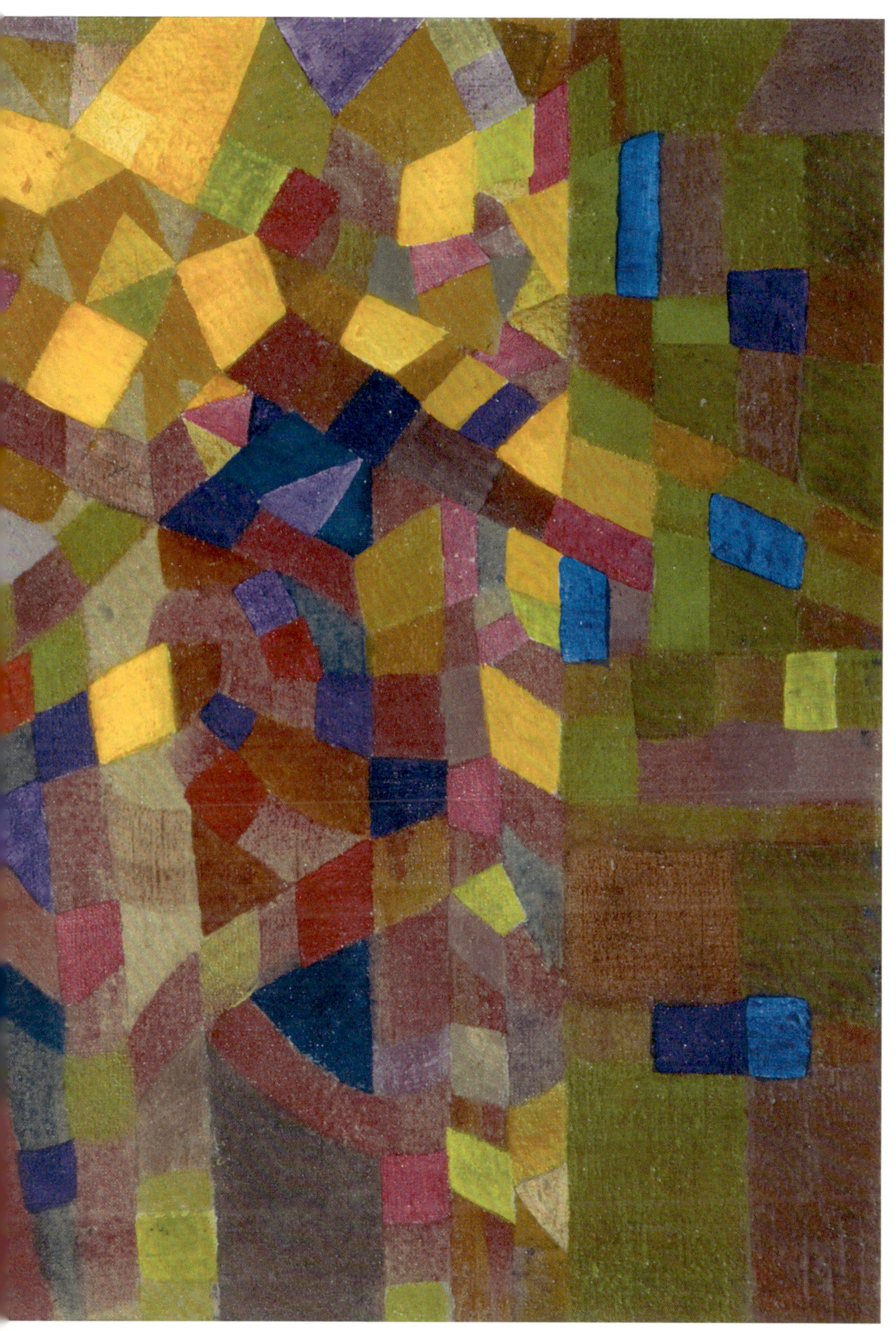

Berta Fischer

Berta Fischer (1973 Germany) is best known for her light, abstract sculptures made of synthetic materials like PVC and acrylic glass. Made in fluorescent colours, her playful works are suspended from the wall or hanging from the ceiling, creating an impression of lightness that is recurrent across her work. Each sculpture made in acrylic glass involves digital modelling, computer-controlled laser cutting and modelling by hand. She describes her process: *'I have always worked with plastics. What is decisive for me is the transparency and the ease with which you can create your own material.'* AGK

Berta Fischer, *Xurla*, 2016
Acrylic glass, 170 × 190 × 75 cm

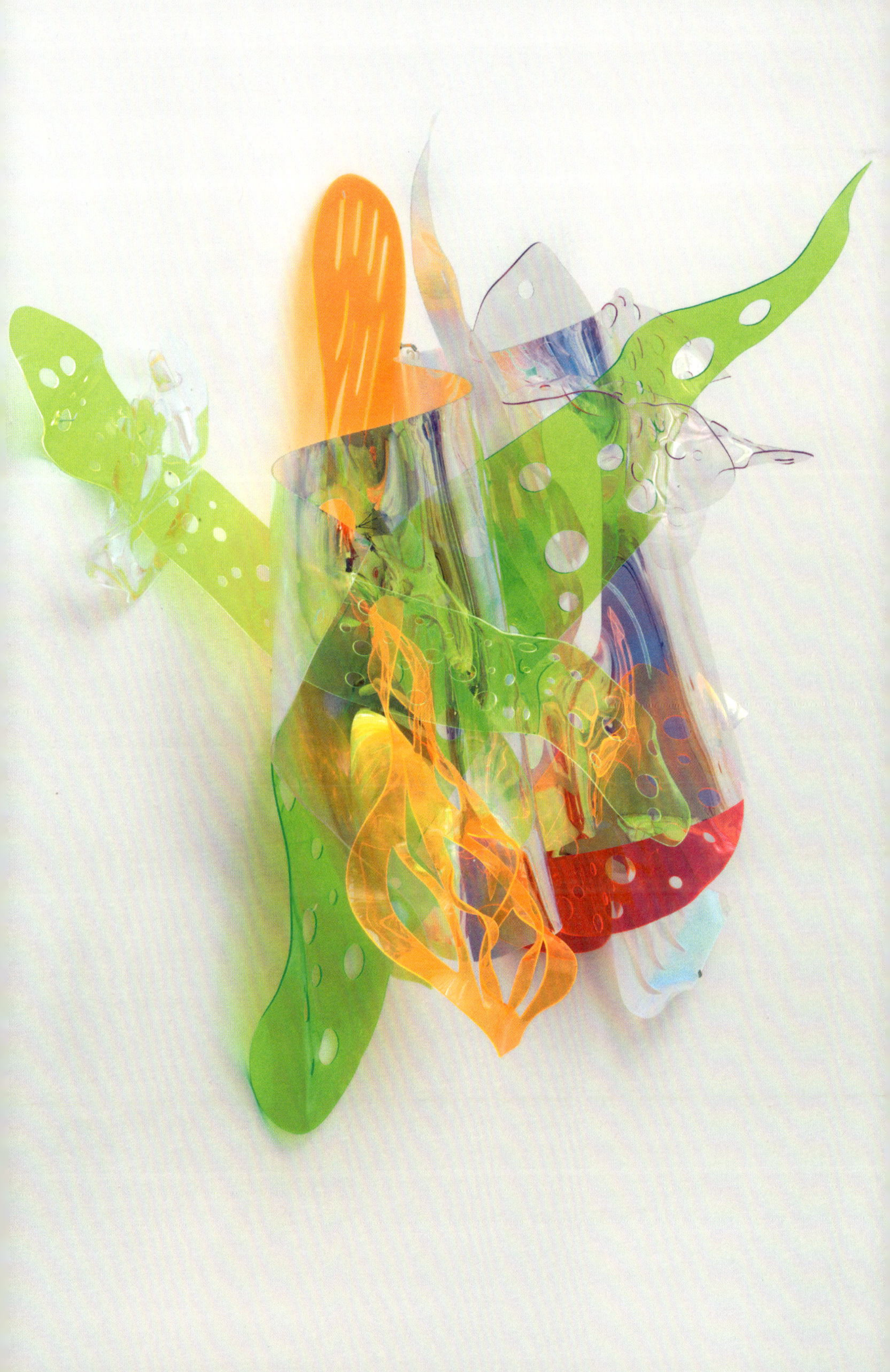

Till Gerhard

Till Gerhard (1971 Germany) works mainly in painting but has also made installations, sculptures, performances and films. Working in the figurative tradition and drawing from the work of artists like Gerhard Richter, Gerhard often finds his starting point in a photograph. To a realistic rendering of this initial image, he then adds expressive splashes or renders of paint. '*I paint from life,*' Gerhard describes, '*the paintings always contain the possibility of beauty and the abyss, showing how thin the ice that we walk on actually is.*' IAK

Till Gerhard, *Black Hole/Sun*, 2007
Oil on canvas, 200 × 165 cm

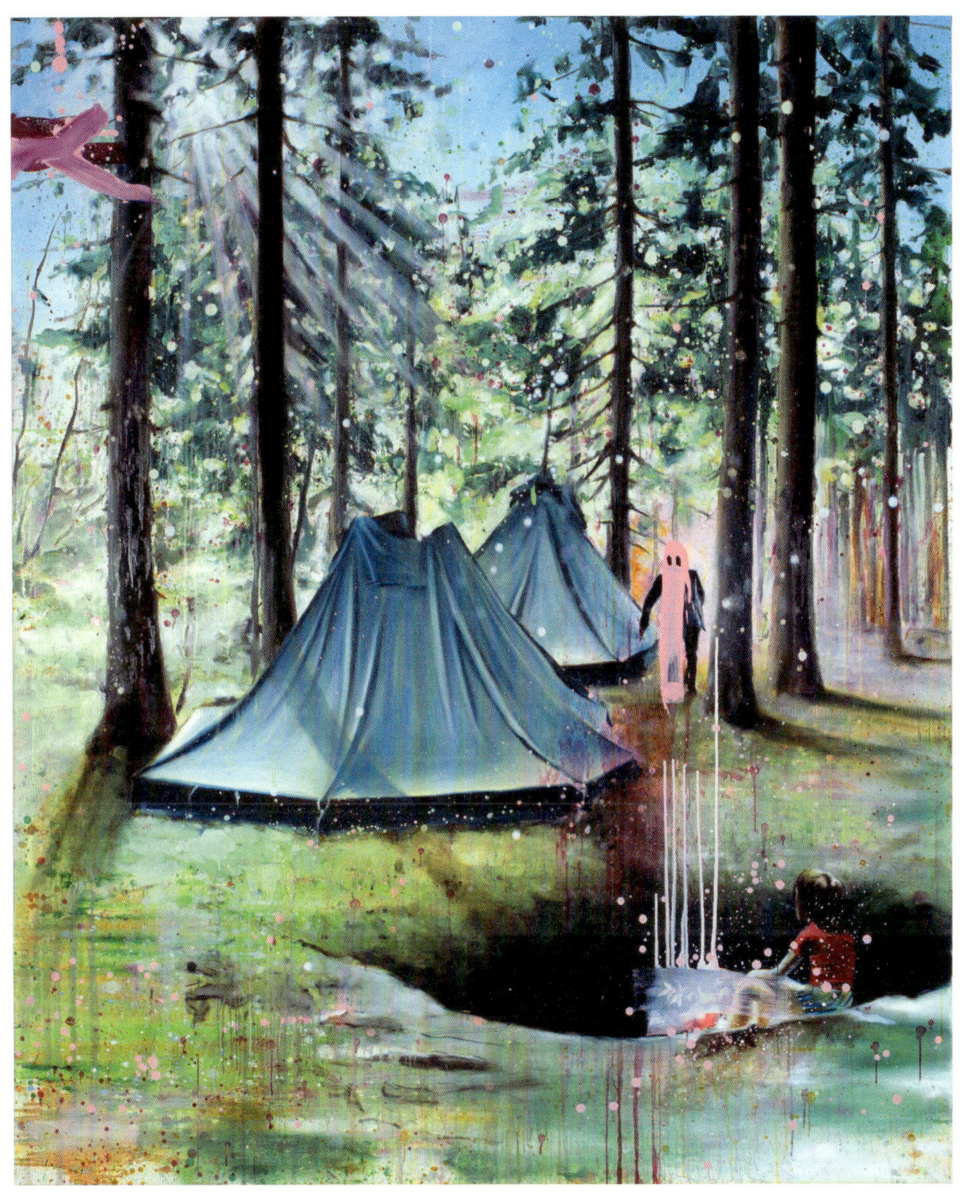

Rodney Graham

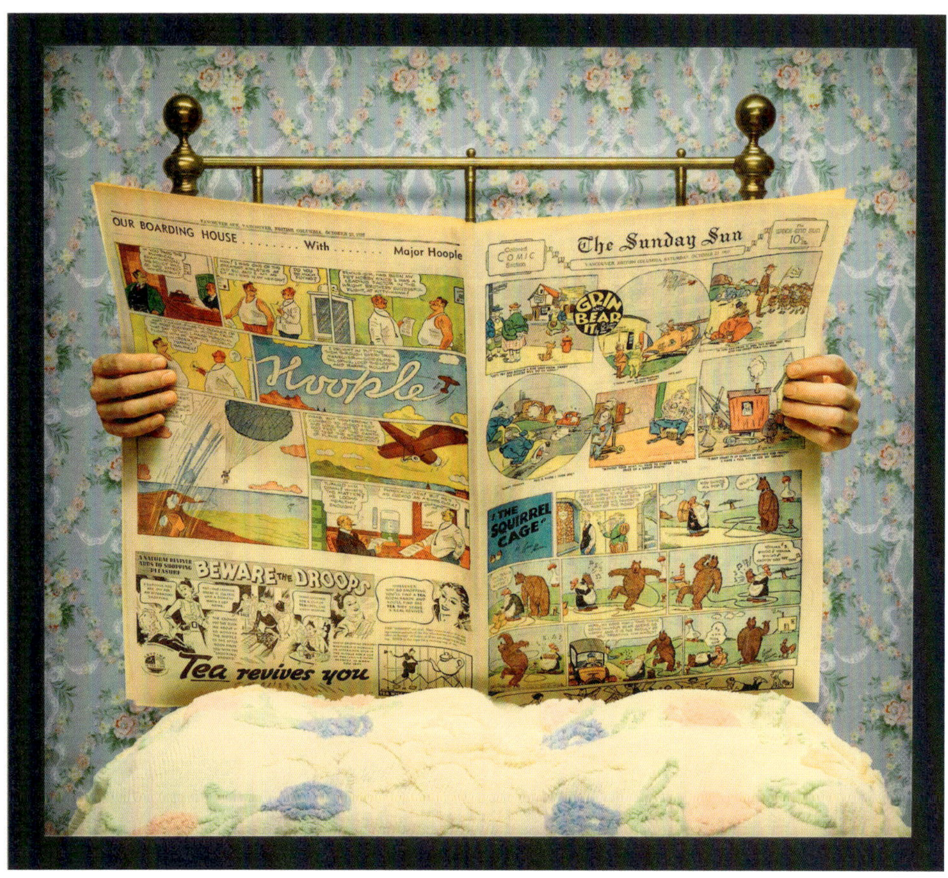

Rodney Graham (1949 Canada) lives and works in Vancouver, Canada. Graham is known for his conceptual photographs, performances, films, sculptures and paintings, which adopt a witty sense of humour to reference tropes in art history, literature, cinema and popular culture. Graham attended the University of British Columbia, where he was taught by the artist Jeff Wall and engaged with the photo-conceptualist scene in 1970s Vancouver. In 1994, Graham began making films of himself which parodied characters like Robinson Crusoe trapped in never-ending loops. In 2003, Graham extended this practice to photography. *It may be a burden to reinvent oneself every time,* Graham has said, *but it makes things more interesting.* cs

Rodney Graham, *Sunday Sun 1937*, 2012
Lightbox transparency, 88 × 88 × 17.8 cm

Thore Heramb

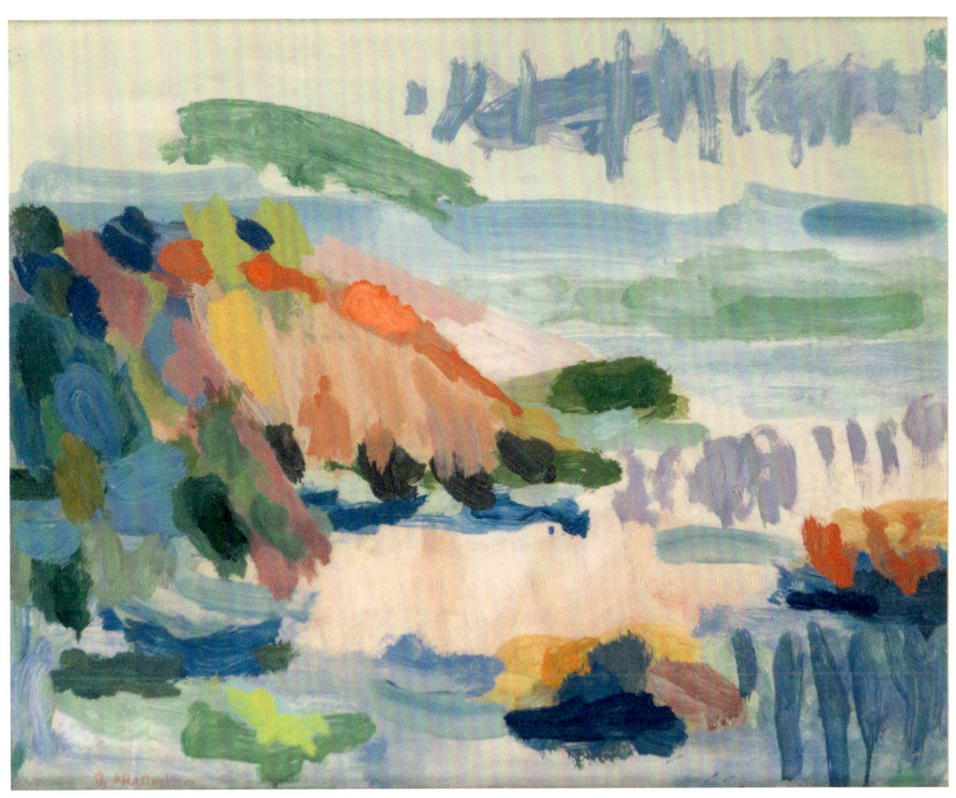

Thore Heramb (1916–2014 Norway) was one of Norway's finest colourists. With his abstract imagery of nature, he became a transitional figure in Norwegian art, bridging the figurative works of the 1930s and the consistently non-figurative painting that came to prominence in the 1950s. Looking at modern French art, his interest in Cubism led to an increasing degree of abstraction and concentration on the construction of the picture space, which he then combined with other influences. *Through the strict demands of constructive art on ability, I have reached a period where Impressionism and Norwegian colouristic landscape art mean a lot to me.'* IAK

Thore Heramb, *Landskapskomposisjon* (Landscape composition), 1958
Oil on board, 50 × 64.5 cm

Paulina Olowska

Paulina Olowska (1976 Poland) lives and works in Rabka-Zdroj, Poland. Like the twentieth-century European avant-gardes, she embraces all aspects of the arts from painting to graphics, fashion, stage and costume design, performance and activism; she even co-founded and designed an artist's bar. Her monumental figurative paintings often feature modern women in magazine-style poses against backdrops of utopian scenarios. *'I like to use fashion in artworks as a tool to speak about past ideologies and allude to different movements and moments in history.'* IB

Paulina Olowska, *Window Display* GUM, 2018
Oil, gouache and acrylic on canvas, 190.5 × 198.1 cm

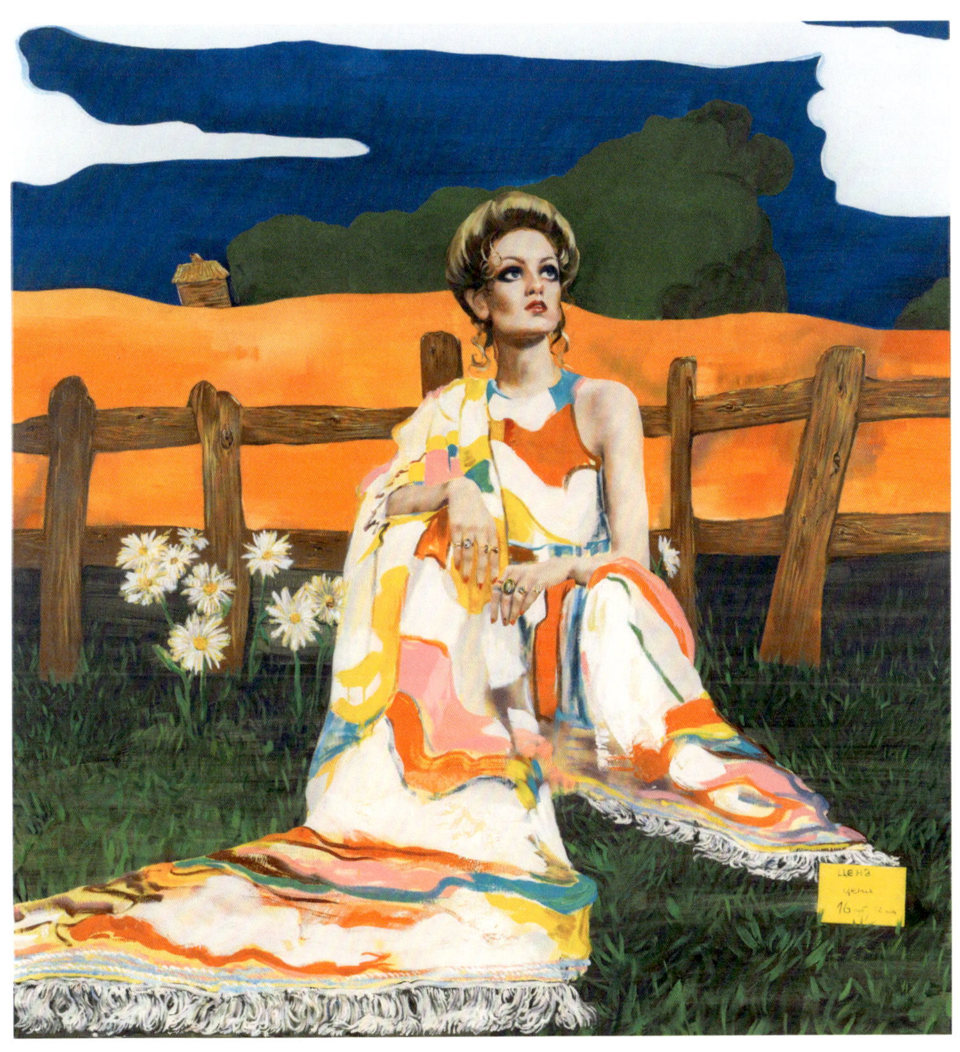

Pierre et Gilles

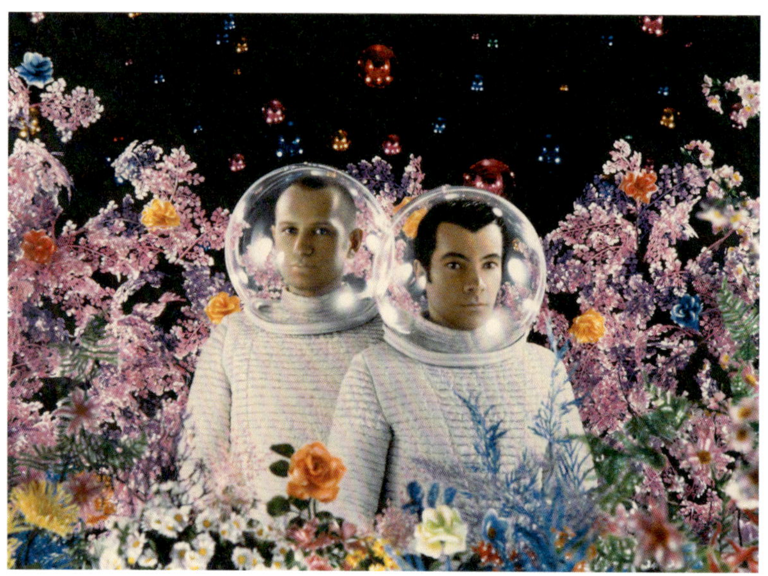

Pierre et Gilles (1950 and 1953 France) is a partnership between Pierre Commoy and Gilles Blanchard, two artists who have been working together since 1976 to blur the conventions between photography and painting. The duo photograph their subjects in their studio, often creating elaborate life-size sets, and then printing the portrait on canvas and applying paint to it. Their work sits at an intersection of fashion photography (iconic sitters have included Jean Paul Gaultier and Madonna) and the pop art movement associated with artists such as David LaChapelle. For the artists, their work is *a family album that evolves all the time*. TM

Pierre et Gilles, *Les Cosmonautes*, 1991
C-print edition after the original work *Les Cosmonautes – Autoportrait*, 1991, 40 × 55 cm

Laura Owens

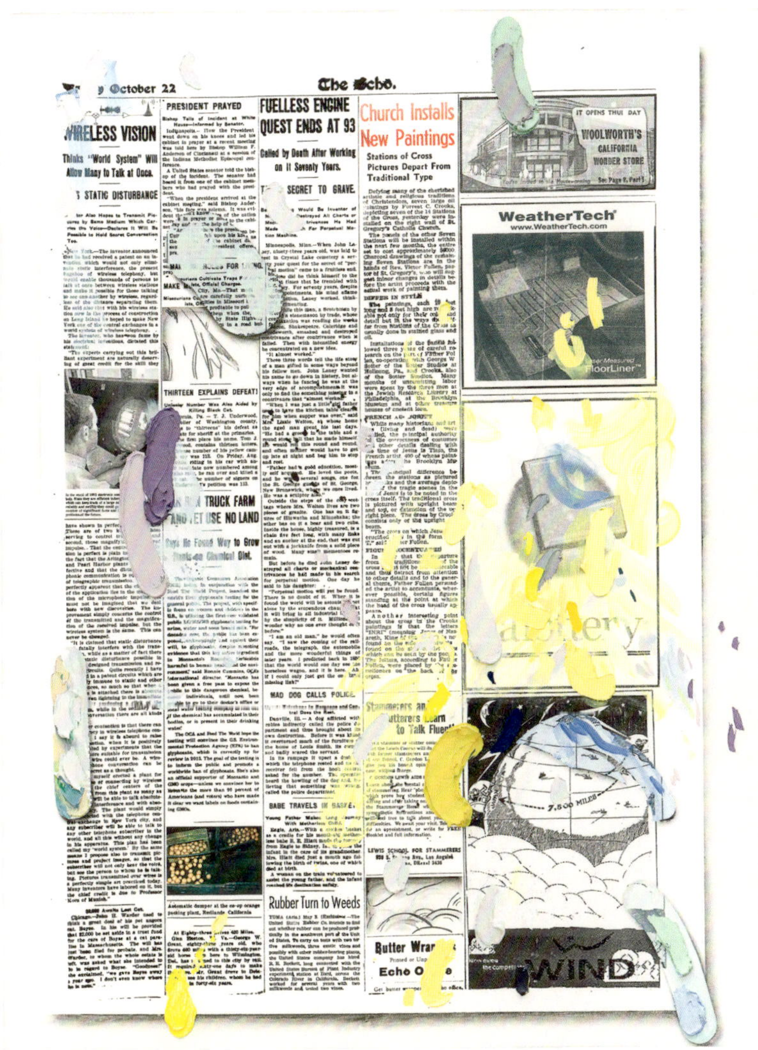

Laura Owens (1970 USA) emerged on the Los Angeles art scene during the 1990s and is best known for large-scale, mixed-media paintings. Throughout her career, Owens has questioned the nature of painting and the painter's process, while refusing to commit to one style or approach. By incorporating personal allusions, sketching and craft materials into her works, she has challenged traditional assumptions about figuration and abstraction. In recent years, she has made use of silk-screening, computer manipulation, digital printing and material exploitation. Owens has said *'each particular painting has a sort of grab bag of places it's coming from, and those get kind of mixed and chopped up and moved around… There's no limit as to what the work is referencing.'* AGK

Laura Owens, *Untitled*, 2015
Oil, silkscreen ink, flashe, charcoal, acrylic and gesso on linen, 351 × 264.2 × 8.5 cm

Johannes Rian

Johannes Rian (1891–1981 Norway) was one of the great Norwegian colourists of his time. He worked as a farmer and dreamt of becoming a violinist before an accident changed the course of his life and he decided to pursue painting at the age of thirty-six. Rian believed there was an ideal placement of forms with ideal accompanying colours, yet he sought to liberate colour from objects. A meeting with Henri Matisse in the south of France in 1950 strong influenced him, which is evident in his works from the 1950s. In the following decades, his motives became more abstract. In 1936, he wrote: *I believe that within the next 25 years, painting will have entered an entirely new phase. I believe the abstract painting will conquer the world.'* AGK

Johannes Rian, *Spansk restaurant* (Spanish restaurant), 1949
Oil on board, 54.5 × 45 cm

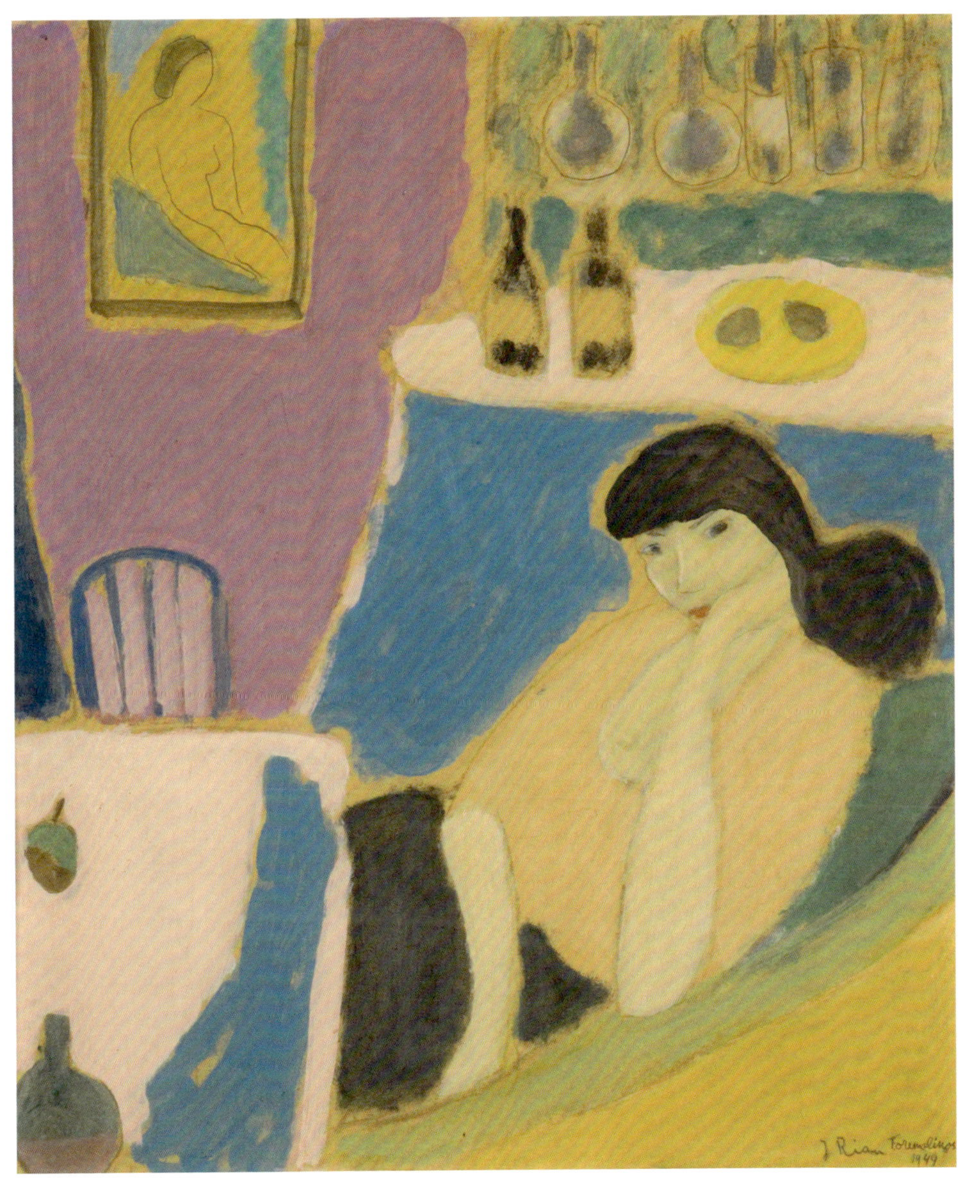

Julia Rommel

Julia Rommel (1980 USA) makes monochromatic and geometric paintings that form a research into colour and the potential within their juxtapositions. Her oil paintings have a strong sense of history in their formal references to the Abstract Expressionism as an example. In recent years, Rommel began removing her canvases from their stretchers, re-stretching them numerous times onto different sized formats in order to imprint borders from their earlier framings. By making the process itself part of the work, the artist draws attention to the materiality and objectiveness of the work. She says, *'I've found myself taking elaborate steps to keep my own signature away.'* TM

Julia Rommel, *Ex-husband*, 2018
Oil on linen, 213.4 × 210.8 cm

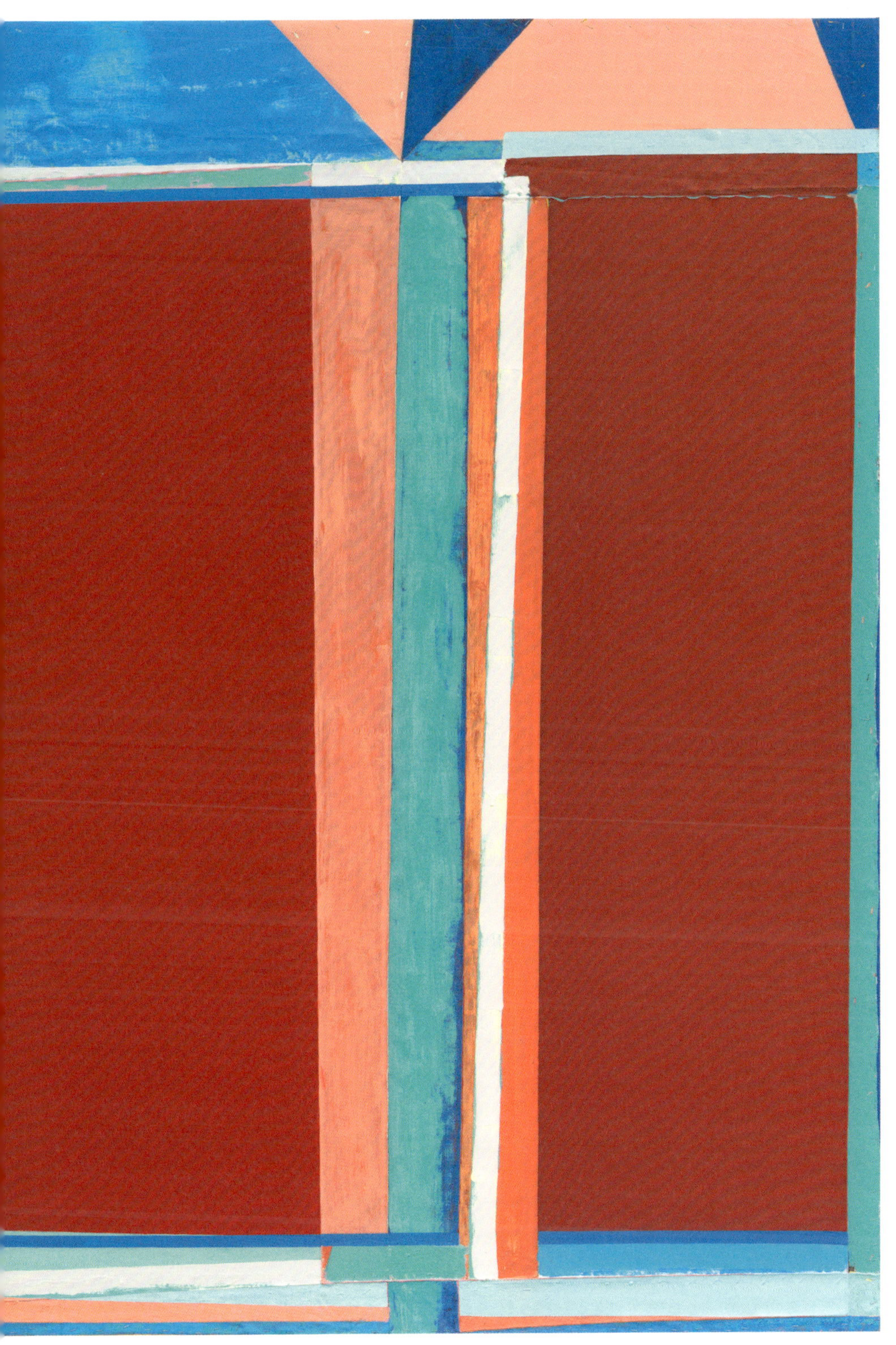

Ed Ruscha

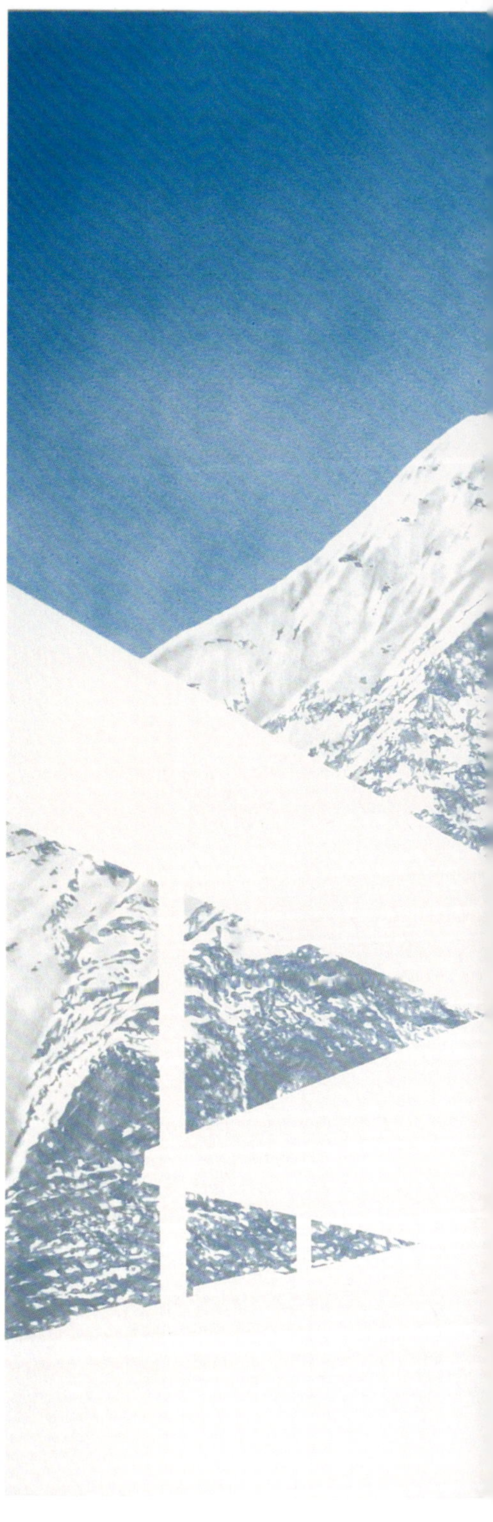

Ed Ruscha (1937 USA) creates conceptual paintings, prints and photo books inspired by the sprawl and the vernacular of his native California, where he studied and works. Billboards, gas stations and LA's entertainment industries provide Ruscha with a vocabulary of phrases and a smooth graphic style that he deploys to express the sublime in the everyday. *I've always been intrigued by oblique perspectives, like aerial views. There's something about the table-top ... taking a viewer up in the air, so you can look down from an angle.'* CS

Ed Ruscha, *Mountain Standard*, 2000
Acrylic on canvas, 163 × 183 cm

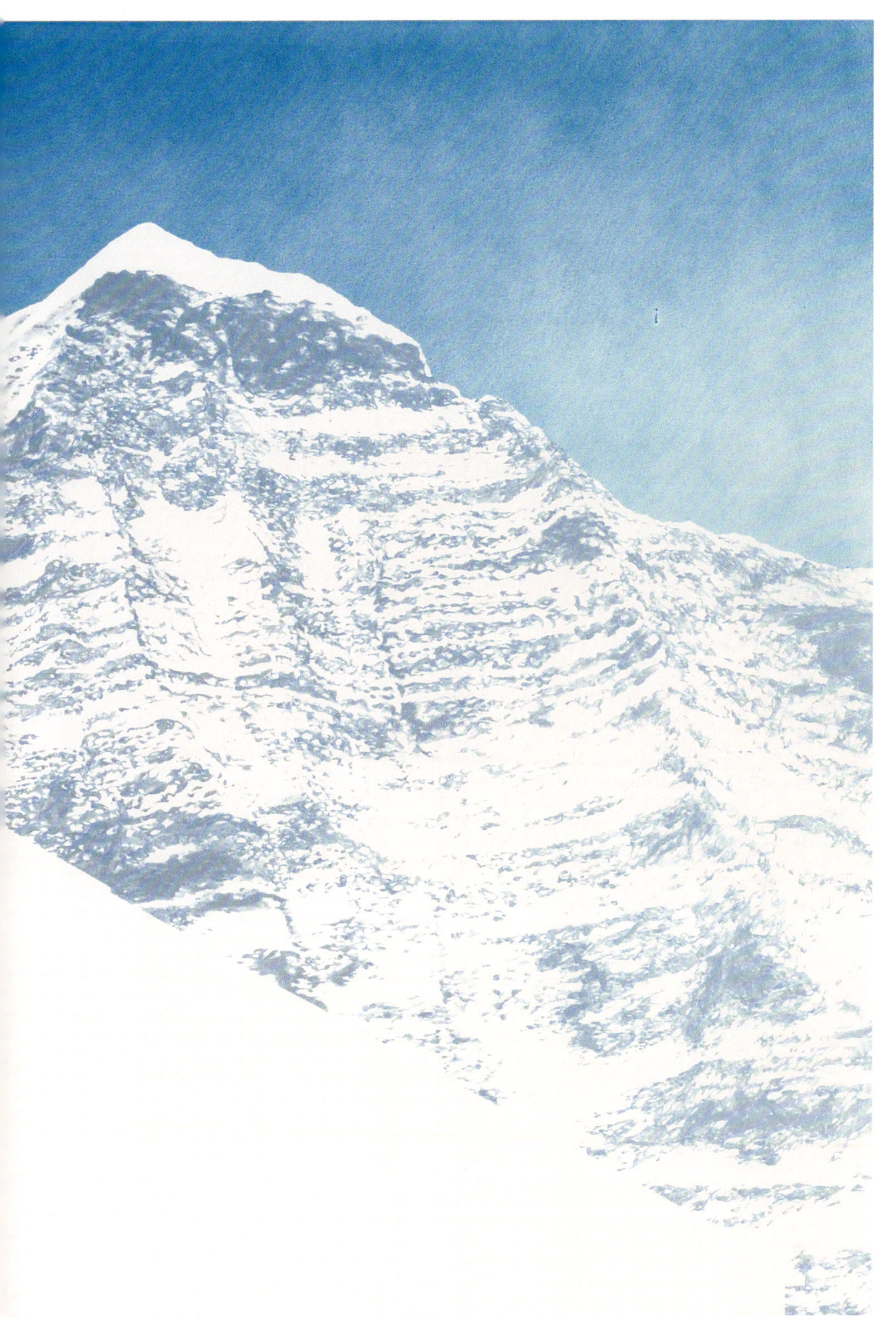

Caragh Thuring

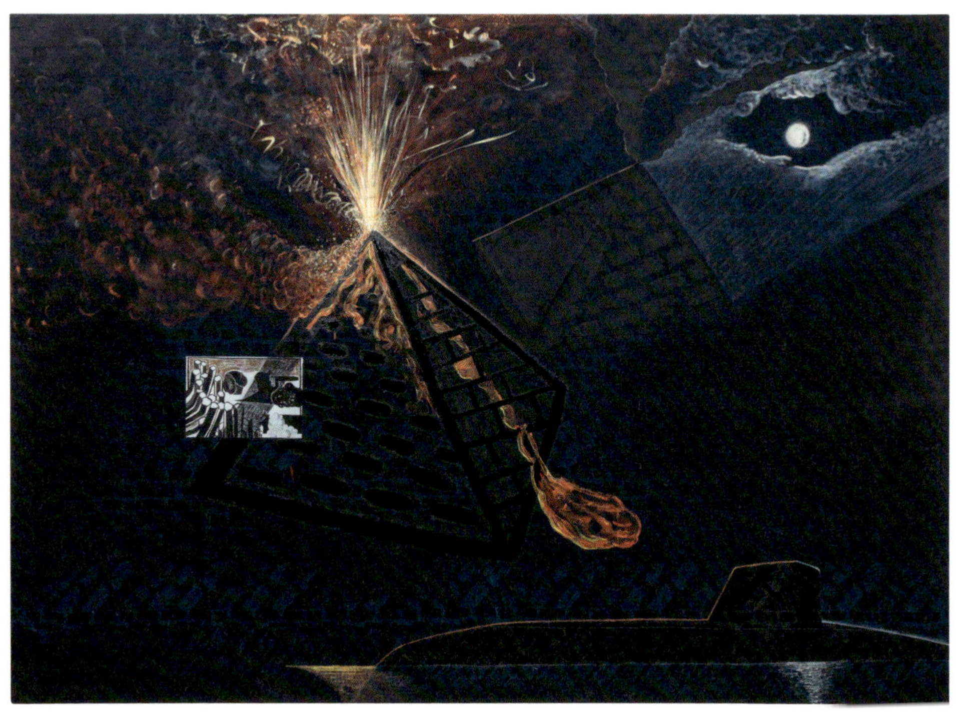

Caragh Thuring (1972 Belgium) lives and works between London, UK and Argyll, Scotland. Thuring is known for working on unprimed linen and bespoke woven cloth comprised of digital renderings of her previous paintings, photographs and found images. The cloths are sewn together and stretched before they are painted. Her paintings feature recurring motifs including the human silhouette, pyramids, brickwork, windows, submarines and volcanoes. She explains, *'I've always been fascinated by their subterranean mystery, and the fact that they destroy themselves as well as build themselves from underneath.'* GS

Caragh Thuring, *Night*, 2017
Oil, pigment, bitumen, gesso, acrylic, graphite, pitt pastel, spray paint,
synthetic indigo, on dyed cotton and linen, 152.4 × 213.36 cm

Skuja Braden

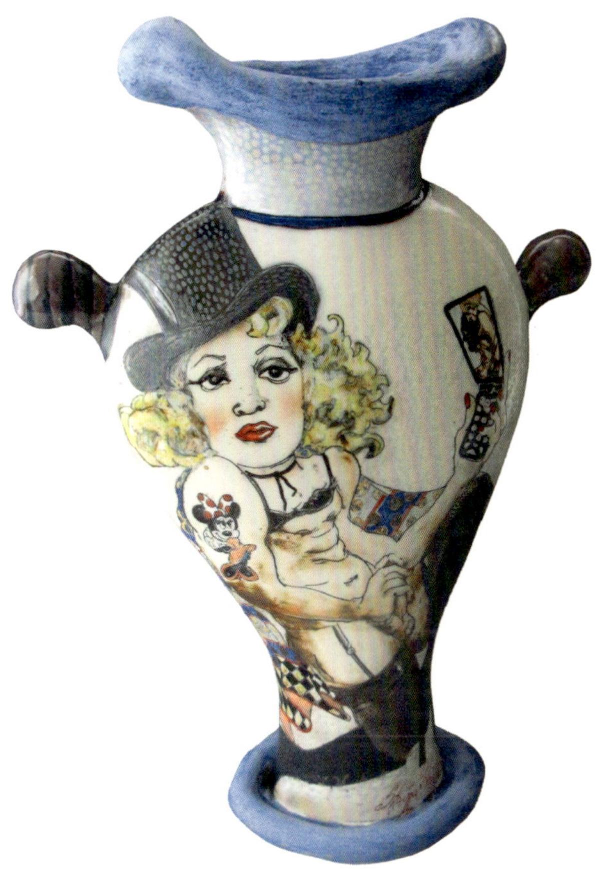

Skuja Braden is the collaborative name of the duo Ingūna Skuja (1965 Latvia) and Melissa Braden (1968 USA) who work primarily with porcelain. Skuja Braden represents an 'absence of presence' of an individual author, where two artists have combined forces and create a fictional alternative proxy identity. The work is conceptually based, but always expressed as a synthesis of painting and sculpture that mixes decorative, literary and political elements into hybrid forms using a material that has historically been associated with sophistication. *'Often, when particularly free-standing vases, one of us is holding, the other one is squeezing together, and then something starts to come apart, then one of us starts yelling, the other one starts yelling, and then we squeeze it together.'* IAK

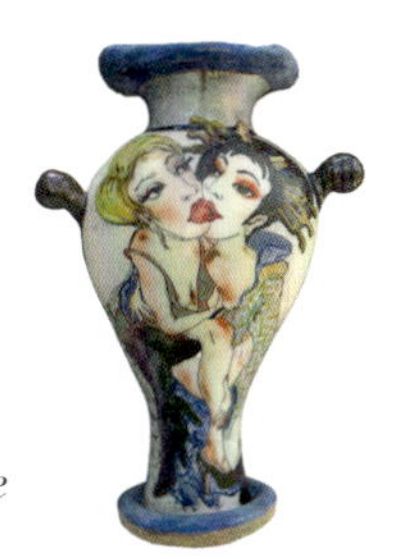

Skuja Braden, *Ima Woman*, 2017
Hand built porcelain, 57 × 42 × 20 cm

Fredrik Værslev

Fredrik Værslev (1979 Norway) is known for his process-oriented practice, which combines meticulous planning and spontaneity. He often uses materials found in domestic life, and his methods include painting on wooden pallets, aging painted canvases outdoors, and painting with a trolley normally used to paint roads and mark the edges of playing fields. Værslev's compositions are influenced by his everyday life and childhood, graphic design and abstract and Minimalist painting. He has said of his process: *'There's this incredibly slow part that happens when dealing with decisions made by Nature; to make the works dry, frost, fade in the sunlight, and age the way I'd like them to. It can easily take months before I apply another brushstroke or a spill that is yet again a decision made in a split second.'* AGK

Fredrik Værslev, *Untitled*, 2018
Primer, spray paint, acrylic, white spirit, cotton canvas on
wooden stretcher and steel construction, 210 × 145.1 × 33.3 cm

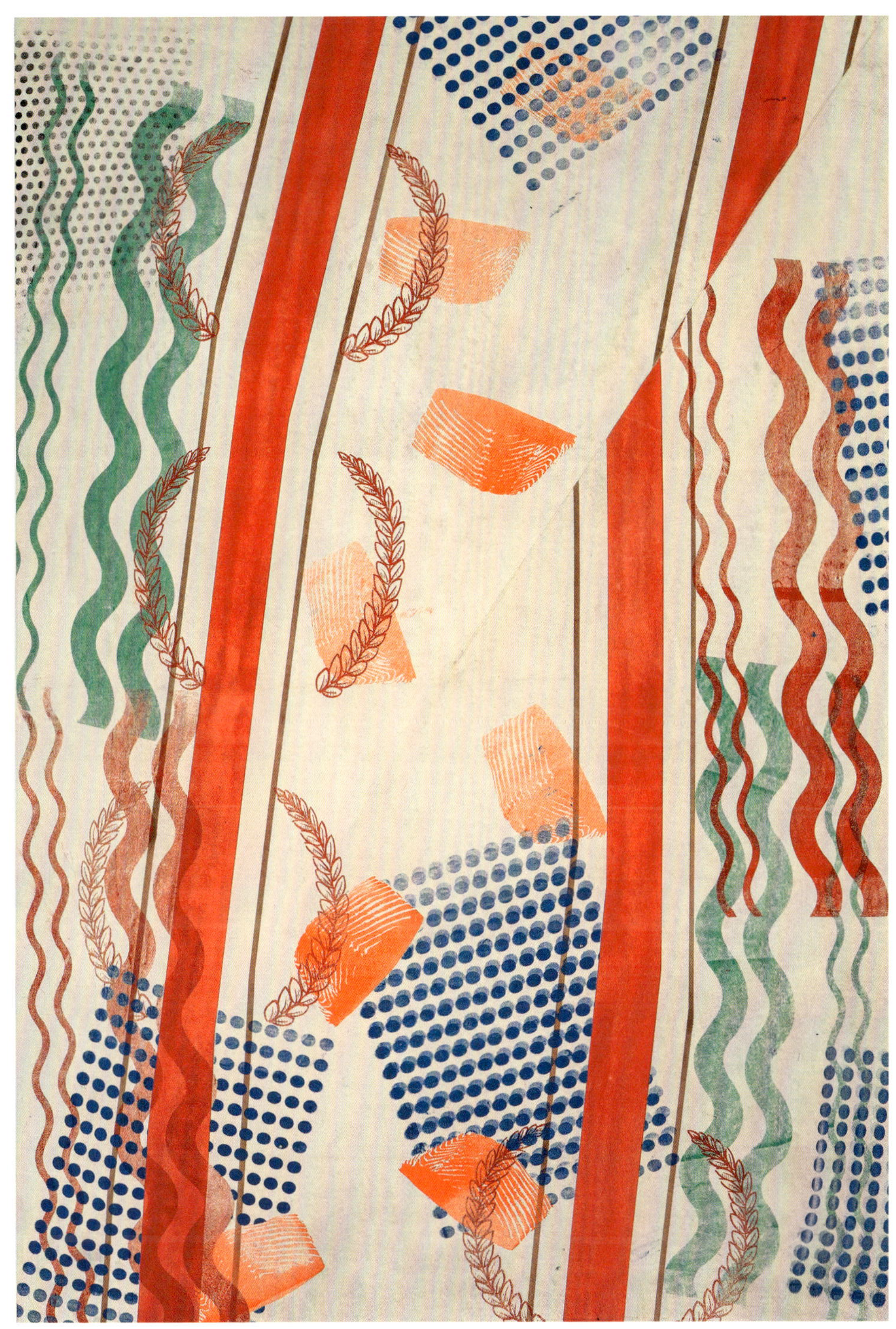

Charline von Heyl

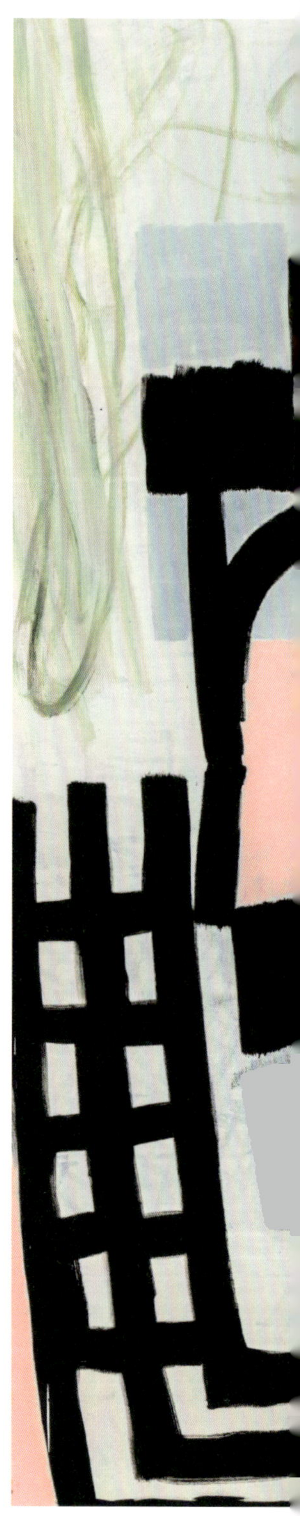

Charline von Heyl (1960 Germany) is a painter who also works in drawing, printmaking and collage. Working between New York and Marfa, Texas, von Heyl's exuberantly coloured canvases are formally diverse with their bold lines and abstract patterns and shapes. Her practice seeks to do away with the conventions embedded within the history of painting from composition and narrative to questions around artistic subjectivity. To do this, von Heyl creates visceral and playful artworks that reference a broad range of topics including metaphysics, pop culture and literature. She says, *'What I want to do with a painting is establish a relationship of now. You know that you are in the moment, in front of painting, and something happens.'* ™

Charline von Heyl, *Stationmaster*, 2013
Acrylic and oil on canvas, 208.3 × 198.1 cm

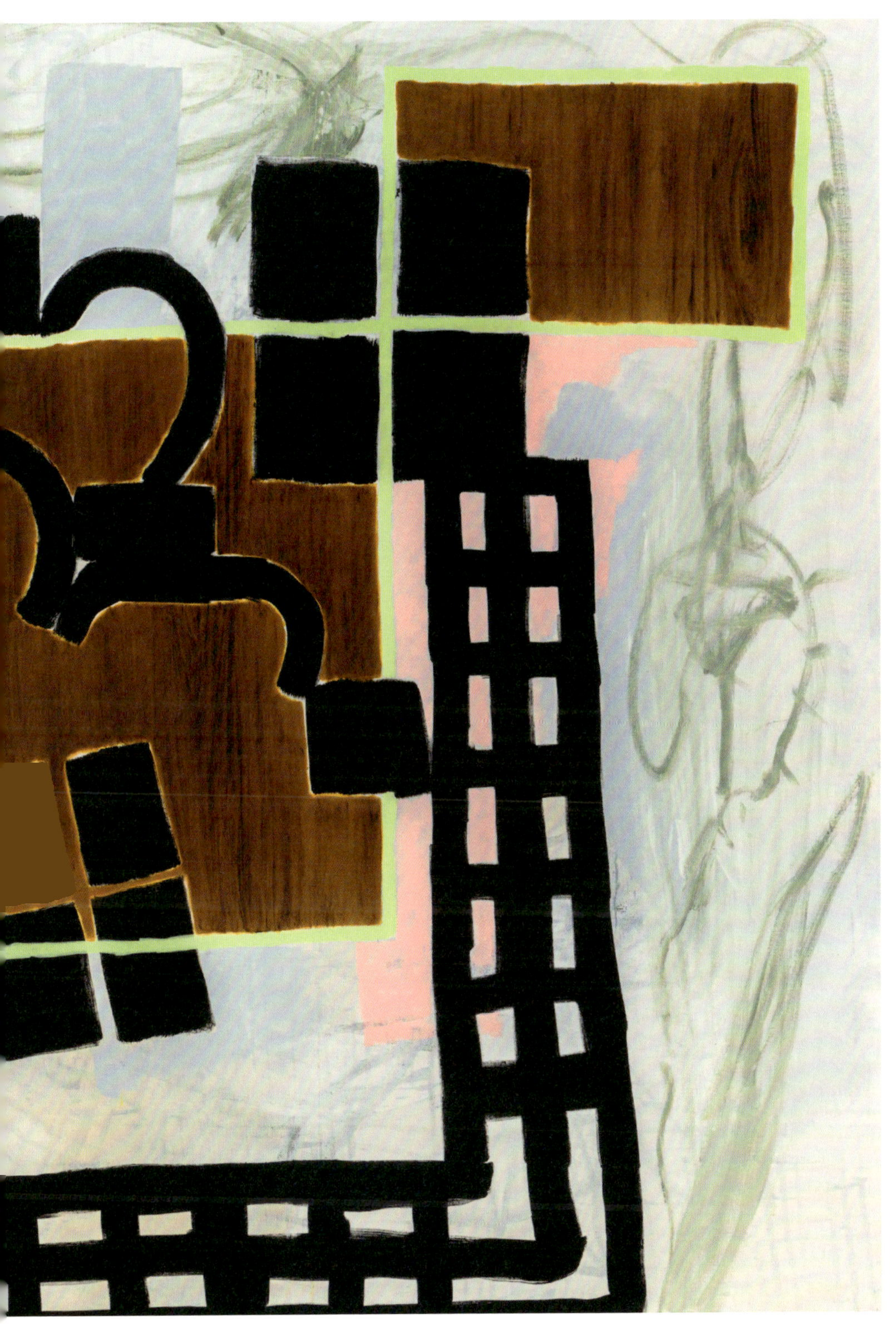

Jakob Weidemann

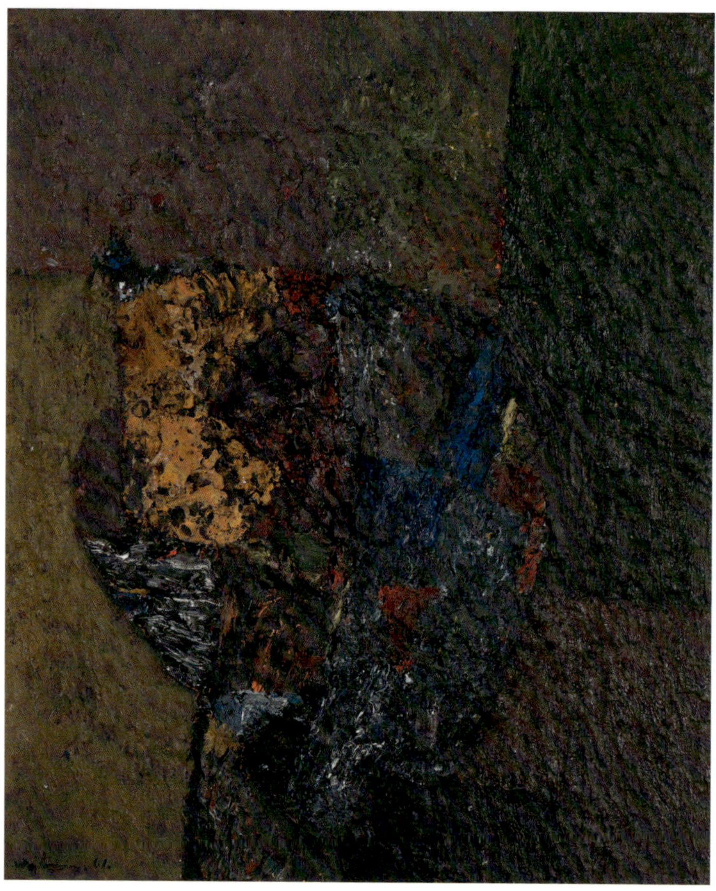

Jakob Weidemann (1923–2001 Norway) played a central role in the breakthrough of abstract painting in Norway. An explosion during World War II led to Weidemann losing sight in his right eye. Following this, a dark and expressive pull came into his pictures in the coming period. Weidemann belonged to the genre of expressive, lyrical-abstract art, where nature provided a source of inspiration and a starting point. He wanted to peel away everything and get down to the core, to the detail in the element itself or to the 'bare bedrock' as he himself called it. *'Beauty is certainly what we know most about. Something has hit us; there is a unique consensus. It only becomes complicated when it comes to the individual's special expression. It's natural. We can be united in one truth, but never think alike. We can agree on a picture, but never see the same thing, and yet we all know what beauty is.'* IAK

Jakob Weidemann, *Fra Skogen* (From the Forest), 1961
Mixed media on board, 69 × 60 cm

Oluf Wold-Torne

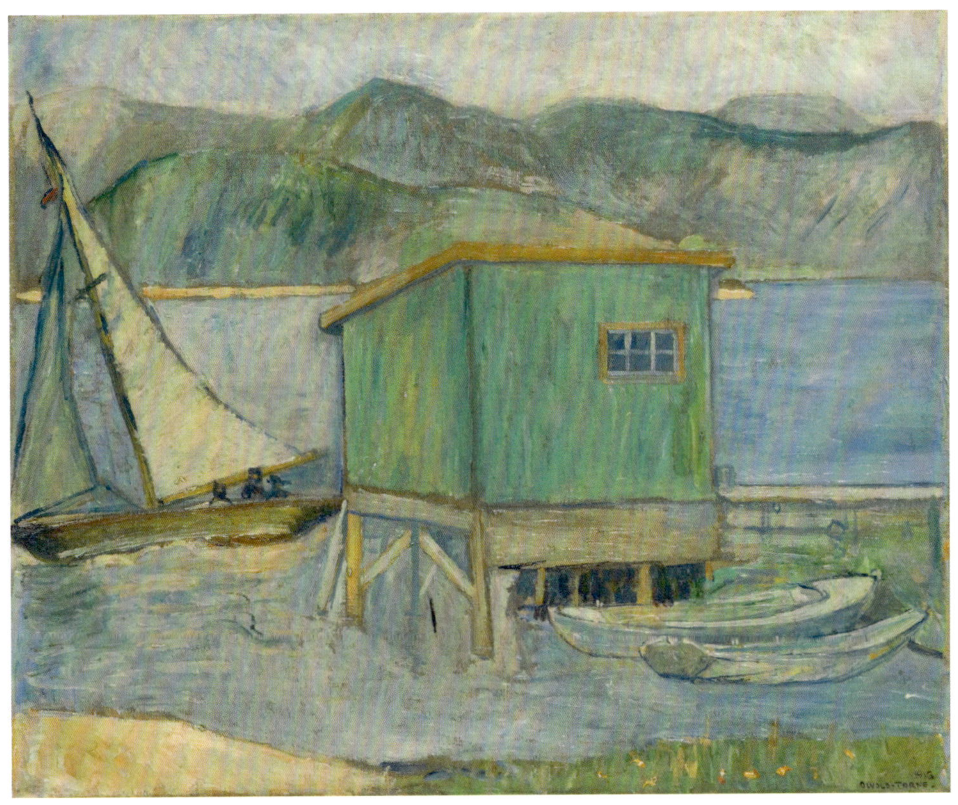

Oluf Wold-Torne (1867–1919 Norway) is sometimes referred to as 'Norway's Cézanne' and is an artist who stands out in Norwegian art history: throughout much of his career, he painted traditional still life motifs, mostly with a vase of flowers and a bowl of apples. His older still lives are often saturated with heavy symbolism that gives each object its own meaning, but for Wold-Torne it is form, colour and the effects of light that are most important. Recognised, with Thorvald Erichsen and Henrik Sørensen, as the 'Holmsbu painters', a group of artists around whom a rich artistic environment and residency developed at the rural village of Holmsbu. *An artist residency at the countryside is not a holiday retreat*', stressed Wold-Torne, who, in his paintings, said he could *'not be allowed to talk to every single flower and nature itself – painting is my only means of coming into God's arms here on earth.'* IAK

Oluf Wold-Torne, *Seilas ved badehus, Holmsbu* (Regatta near a bath house, Holmsbu), 1913
Oil on canvas, 50 × 62 cm

List of Works

p.75

LAURA OWENS
Untitled, 2015
Oil, silkscreen ink, flashe,
charcoal, acrylic and gesso on
linen
351 × 264.2 × 8.5 cm

p.77

JOHANNES RIAN
Spansk restaurant
(Spanish restaurant), 1949
Oil on board
54.5 × 45 cm

pp.78–9

JULIA ROMMEL
Ex-husband, 2018
Oil on linen
213.4 × 210.8 cm

pp.80–1

ED RUSCHA
Mountain Standard, 2000
Acrylic on canvas
163 × 183 cm

p.82

CARAGH THURING
Night, 2017
Oil, pigment, bitumen, gesso,
acrylic, graphite, pitt pastel,
spray paint, synthetic indigo,
on dyed cotton and linen
152.4 × 213.36 cm

p.83

SKUJA BRADEN
Ima Woman, 2017
Hand built porcelain
57 × 42 × 20 cm

p.85

FREDRIK VÆRSLEV
Untitled, 2018
Primer, spray paint, acrylic,
white spirit, cotton canvas on
wooden stretcher and steel
construction
210 × 145.1 × 33.3 cm

pp.86–7

CHARLINE VON HEYL
Stationmaster, 2013
Acrylic and oil on canvas
208.3 × 198.1 cm

p.88

JAKOB WEIDEMANN
Fra Skogen (From the Forest),
1961
Mixed media on board
69 × 60 cm

p.89

OLUF WOLD-TORNE
Seilas ved badehus, Holmsbu
(Regatta near a bath house,
Holmsbu), 1913
Oil on canvas
50 × 62 cm

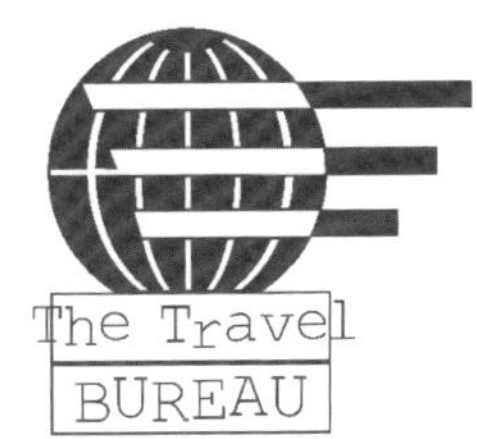

Acknowledgements

The Whitechapel Gallery would like to thank the generosity of Christen Sveaas and the team at Christen Sveaas Art Foundation for their commitment and support in making this collaboration possible and for allowing this wonderful collection to travel to London. Our thanks to William Flatmo, Director, Anja Grøner Krogstad, Assistant Director and Idunn Yr Alman-Kaas, Artistic Coordinator/ Registrar for sharing their exceptional knowledge, expertise and enthusiasm.

Our gratitude and admiration extend to Paulina Olowska for accepting our invitation and imagining this beautiful display. We also extend our thanks to the team at Simon Lee Gallery, London for their invaluable assistance and guidance: Will Davies, Cristina Herraiz Peleteiro, Georgia Lurie, Elena Rueda and to the team at Pace Gallery for their support: Kate Brownbill, Karine Haimo and Adam Rutledge. Special thanks also Viktoriia Semenska for her help and support and to Sabine Breitwieser for her editorial assistance.

Paulina Olowska would like to thank all of the artists included in her display, alongside Delia Gonzalez, Laura Grudniewska, Noah Mclean, Ryan Muller, Bartosz Przybył-Olowski, Urszula Palusinska, Sylwia Rams-Pikuła and Agata Przyborska.

The Whitechapel Gallery would like to thank its supporters, whose generosity enables the Gallery to realise its pioneering programmes.

The exhibition is also generously supported by:

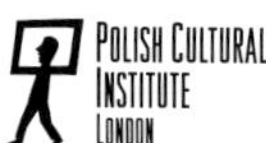

TOWARDS TOMORROW CHAMPIONS
D. Daskalopoulos Collection
Michael and Nina Zilkha

MAJOR DONORS
Asymmetry Art Foundation
Bloomberg Philanthropies
City Bridge Trust
Clore Cultural Learning Fund
Collezione Maramotti
Max Mara
NEON
Swarovski Foundation

EXHIBITIONS PROGRAMME
The AKO Foundation
Aldgate Connect BID
Bagri Foundation
Balice Hertling, Paris
Jill & Jay Bernstein
Christen Sveaas Art Foundation
Cockayne Grants for the Arts
Nicoletta Fiorucci Russo
Gagosian
Gladstone Gallery
Sarah & Gerard Griffin
Oliver Haarmann
Henry Moore Foundation
Hiscox
Marguerite Steed Hoffman
Galerie Hubert Winter, Vienna
Institut für Auslandsbeziehungen
Lietta & Dakis Joannou
Karma International, Zürich
kaufmann repetto, Milan, New York
The Klimt Charitable Trust
Galerie Lelong & Co.
London Community Foundation
Galerie Neu, Berlin
The Norwegian Embassy
Idan & Batia Ofer
Polish Cultural Institute, London
Regen Projects
Ellen & Michael Ringier
Emmanuel Roman
Marco Rossi
Alex Sainsbury

Allan Schwartzman
Beth Swofford
Galerie Tanit Munich-Beirut
Laura & Barry Townsley
TRAMPS New York and London
V-A-C Foundation
Michael Werner Gallery
The Whitechapel Gallery
    Commissioning Council
White Cube
and those who wish to remain anonymous

EDUCATION & COMMUNITY PROGRAMMES
Aldgate Connect BID
Art Fund
The Arts Society Westminster
Dorota & Olivier Audemars
Capital Group
Clore Cultural Learning Fund
Paul Hamlyn Foundation
Mayor of London
Newham Council Enrichment
Programme
ZVM Rangoonwala Foundation
Dasha Shenkman
Swarovski Foundation
The London Borough of Tower Hamlets
The Worshipful Company of Grocers

PUBLIC EVENTS PROGRAMME
Aldgate Connect BID
The London Borough of Tower Hamlets
City of London Corporation
Genesis Kickstart Fund, Genesis
Foundation
Stanley Picker Trust

CAPITAL RENEWAL PROGRAMME
The Headley Trust
Culture Recovery Fund, Heritage
Stimulus Fund – Historic England
The Wolfson Foundation

WHITECHAPEL GALLERY CORPORATE
    PATRONS AND MEMBERS
Bloomberg Philanthropies
Frasers Property UK
Gazelli Art House
Phillips
David Zwirner

WHITECHAPEL GALLERY
    CORPORATE SUPPORTERS
Aldgate Connect BID
Bloomberg Philanthropies
Burgess & Leigh
Champagne Castelnau
Crozier Fine Arts
FRAME London (Framing Partner)
Hiscox (Artworks Insurance Partner)
Max Mara
Collezione Maramotti
Omni Colour (Signage Partner)
Phillips

FUTURE FUND
Mahera & Mohammad Abu Ghazaleh
Sirine & Ahmad Abu Ghazaleh
Swantje Conrad
Mr Dimitris Daskalopoulos
Maryam & Edward Eisler
Luigi Maramotti
NEON
Dominic Palfreyman
Catherine Petitgas
John Smith and Vicky Hughes
V-A-C Foundation
Sir Siegmund Warburg's Voluntary
Settlement
Arts Council England Catalyst
Endowment Fund

WHITECHAPEL GALLERY
    COMMISSIONING COUNCIL
Dorota Audemars
Erin Bell
Heloisa Genish
Leili Huth
Irene Panagopoulos
Mariela Pissioti
Nicole Saikalis Bay
Alex Sainsbury

WHITECHAPEL GALLERY PATRONS' CHAIR
Francis Outred

WHITECHAPEL GALLERY GLOBAL CIRCLE
Elyse and Lawrence B. Benenson
    Charitarian Foundation
Yan Du
Peter and Maria Kellner
Elie Khouri Art Foundation
and those who wish to remain anonymous

WHITECHAPEL GALLERY STAFF

Iwona Blazwick, *Director*
Tony Stevenson, *Managing Director*

Syara Ahmed, Christopher Aldgate, Henry Allington-Wood, Daniel Allison, Sadika Begum, Olivia Blyth , Connie Butler, Janine Catalano, Ying Tung Chan, Daisy Chan, Emily Church, Miles Clemson, Elizabeth Clowes, Inês Costa, Sarah Crocker, Helen Davison, Tallulah de Castro-Gray, Chloe Dennis, Asa Desouza-Jones, Evangelia Dimitrakopoulou, Sue Evans, Misha Farrant, Shirin Fathi, Cameron Foote, Siobhán Forshaw, Wells Fray-Smith, Claire Gallagher, Farnaz Gholami, Saba Giani, Natalia Gomolka, Tim Gosden, Luke Gregory-Jones, Isabella Griffin, Shani Haquin-Gerade, Jess Heritage, Molly Ingleby, Smitha Islam, Emma Izard, Claire Jensen, Woo Jin Joo, Isobel Keig, Rosie Kennedy, Hana Khan, Fatima Khatun, Jenny Lea, Ryszard Lewandowski, Ruth Lie, Malgorzata Lisiecka, Marthe Lisson, Lauren Lockett, Kirsty Lowry, Tarini Malik, Imaan Marker, Richard Martin, Josiah McNeil, Megan Miller, Glen Moxon, Paul Kenealy, Andia Newton, Amelia Oakley, Justine Pearsall, Ruth Piper, Agostino Quaranta, Holly Robertson, Jane Scarth, Fatemi Seyedeharmaghan, Laura Smith, Vicky Steer, Candy Stobbs, Grace Storey, Allan Struthers, James Sutton, Bea Taylor Searle, Alice Thompson, Alice Thomson, Pia Tolles, Marta Tworkiewicz , Caterina Vaglio-Tessitore, Francesca Vinter, Filine Wagner, Sam Williams, Yuk Wun Jade Wong, Monica Yam, Lydia Yee, Nayia Yiakoumaki, Krasimira Yosifova

We remain grateful for the ongoing support of Whitechapel Gallery Members.

The Whitechapel Gallery is proud to be a National Portfolio Organisation of Arts Council England.

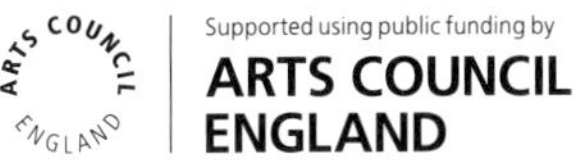

Published on the occasion of the exhibition at the Whitechapel Gallery:

Christen Sveaas Art Foundation:
The Travel Bureau
Selected by Paulina Olowska
14 January–8 May 2022

EXHIBITION
WHITECHAPEL GALLERY
Director: Iwona Blazwick
Assistant Curator: Grace Storey
Head of Exhibition Design and
    Production: Christopher Aldgate
Gallery Technical Manager:
    Ryszard Lewandowski

CHRISTEN SVEAAS
    ART FOUNDATION
Director: William Flatmo
Assistant Director /
    Collection Management:
    Anja Grøner Krogstad
Researcher/Writer:
    Idunn Yr Alman-Kaas

PUBLICATION
Editors: Iwona Blazwick
    with Grace Storey
Head of Publications:
    Francesca Vinter
Copy Editor: Orit Gat
Design: Mark El-khatib
Printed by Pureprint

ISBN 978-0-85488-301-1

First published 2022 by Whitechapel Gallery, London © 2022 Whitechapel Gallery and the authors

Whitechapel Gallery
77–82 Whitechapel High Street
London E1 7QX
whitechapelgallery.org

Distributed by
Thames & Hudson
181a High Holborn
London WC1V 7QX
Tel: +44 (0) 20 7845 5000
sales@thameshudson.co.uk

This publication has been generously supported by Christen Sveaas Art Foundation.

Inside back cover:
Harald Damsleth, poster for
Norwegian State Railways, 1937

Christen Sveaas'
Kunststiftelse

Whitechapel
Gallery